To Peggy,

Assistant Professor
and wondrous
facilitator in our
writing tribe.

Gratefully,

Jan

6/2/11

MAKE YOUR MIND WORK
for you

NEW
MIND-POWER TECHNIQUES
TO IMPROVE MEMORY,
BEAT PROCRASTINATION,
INCREASE ENERGY,
AND MORE!

JOAN MINNINGER, Ph.D.
Author of *Total Recall*
and
ELEANOR DUGAN

Rodale Press, Emmaus, Pennsylvania

Book design by Acey Lee

Library of Congress Cataloging-in-Publication Data

Minninger, Joan.
     Make your mind work for you.

     Includes index.
     1. Mind and body.   2. Thought and thinking.
I. Dugan, Eleanor.   II. Title.
BF161.M57   1988   158′.1   88-18341
ISBN 0-87857-782-3

2 4 6 8 10 9 7 5 3   hardcover

To Dr. George F. Simons

To the Reader

This book is the result of a close collaboration between two authors, even though you will find many experiences described in the first person singular throughout. Each of us was directly involved in the writing and/or evaluating of every sentence. We thought of using the editorial "we" for the stories, but we soon saw that it was awkward and it seemed too impersonal. We decided that using "I" suited the tone of the book better. Just so you will know who is speaking: The first person therapy and seminar stories are by me, Joan Minninger; the first person stories involving the arts are by me, Eleanor Dugan.

CONTENTS

ACKNOWLEDGMENTS

Knowledge is a chain; our chain began with George F. Simons's excited response to Robert Ornstein's new way of thinking about human behavior in his book *Multimind*, which led us to Howard Gardner and his elegant theory of multiple intelligences described in his *Frames of Mind*.

INTRODUCTION
OUR MULTIPLE MINDS

The human mind is stubbornly inefficient, infuriatingly inconsistent, and a rather primitive tool for coping with the world today. It is a holdover from our prehistoric ancestors, perfectly adequate for avoiding saber-toothed tigers and learning to rub two sticks together, but hardly suitable for the Space Age. Yet the simplest mind today controls dazzling skills, the very same skills that put the universe itself within our grasp.

Why this contradiction? Because we possess at least *five major* "minds" in one *mental system,* each highly effective for dealing with different parts of our lives. These multiple "minds" work as a team. Sometimes they rocket along in perfect unison. At other times they are out of synchronization, quarreling among themselves and even sabotaging each other.

A popular concept today is that computers "think" better than people do, faster, more efficiently, and without muddled emotions. Actually, our minds work successfully *because* they are disorganized and redundant. Despite (or perhaps because of) their imperfection, our minds possess three irreplaceable and uniquely human qualities that can never be equaled by computers:

1. They are *adaptable.*

2. They experience *pleasure.*

3. They have a sense of *humor.*

It is these three characteristics that guarantee the survival of the human race.

WHAT MAKES UP
YOUR MIND?

I can't get started. I procrastinate.

I can't concentrate as much as I should.

I get confused and nervous, feel overwhelmed.

I know I should be doing things differently, but I just can't seem to change.

Case histories from a psychiatrist's notebook? Not necessarily. Most of us have uttered one or more of those statements as we cope with the millions of choices and bits of information that flood us every day. The wonder is not that we sometimes fail, but that we do so well!

Stan gets up on a Saturday morning, feeling a great sense of freedom and power. He is free to do whatever he wants until bedtime Sunday night. Of course he's already scheduled some of that precious time away from the office for an exercise class, a visit to relatives, and a club meeting.

He also wants to clean out the basement, get his car repaired, start on his income tax, attend religious services, and catch up on his reading.

He doesn't know it yet, but during the weekend he will be urged to run for president of his club, to lend money to his brother-in-law, to contribute to a telephone charity, to trade in his car for a new one, to try a new cereal he saw advertised on TV, to go to a spur-of-the-moment Saturday night party, and to drive a neighbor to the hospital after a minor accident.

Sound something like the tangle of decisions and choices that you face every day? How do you choose? How do you make up your mind?

Fortunately, you have predecided some things. Your values will provide an automatic "yes" or "no" to some of the choices. You have "programmed" yourself to save time. (You needn't decide hundreds of times a day whether to stay clothed, walk upright, or eat books.)

But sometimes Stan comes to a dead stop and can't decide what to do:

"The party sounds great, but maybe I should stay home and work on my taxes."

"The party sounds like an awful bore, but if I don't go I'll miss the opportunity to . . . "

Or he feels he *should* have the car checked or exercise or go to religious services, but somehow other things always seem to get in the way. He recognizes he's not doing what he thinks he *wants* to do, what he is *supposed* to do. This makes him confused and irritated: "What's wrong with me? Maybe if I had more self-discipline, if I tried harder, if . . . "

Many of us find that there is a difference between what we know we should do and what we actually do: "I know I should quit smoking." "I know I should be better informed about politics." "I know I should manage my money better." Knowing isn't doing. Our mind seems to be powerless to carry out orders in the face of conflicting demands. What sabotages us? How can you take control? How can you make the various parts of your mind work for you, instead of against you?

KNOW YOUR OWN MIND

Your mind is not just a brain. The human being is an information processing system. Therefore, the entire human being is a "mind." It's made up of all of our neural system and every cell and part of our body. So it's not a case of body versus mind—our entire being makes up our mind.

We do two distinct things when we use our mind to process information:

1. We notice. We ask, "What is this?" "What shall I do about it?"

2. We respond. We give commands, ordering the system into action and sending appropriate messages to other parts of the system—chemical messages, mechanical messages, and electrical messages. We do this on both the conscious and unconscious level.

Each of the five parts of our mind can operate at both the conscious level and unconscious level. In most cases, one level is no better than the other, but we use different labels for the process:

The unconscious mind gives and gets *messages*.
The conscious mind has *conversations*.

For example, while our conscious mind is talking to itself— "Which road shall I take?"—our unconscious mind is engrossed in an ill-fitting shoe and decides to send out a protective layer of fluid. It's not until the sensations in our foot register as pain that our conscious mind takes notice. Then the conscious mind starts a different conversation with itself: "What shall I do about this blister?"

If you are fleeing a bear, your conscious mind will probably decide to postpone action and forget the blister in response to the adrenaline rush of the chase. If you are tired and unthreatened, it may decide you should sit down and take off the shoe. Sometimes the conscious mind decides you should ignore the blister under the circumstances: You're on a forced midnight march in basic training

—You're walking down the aisle at your wedding—You're in the middle of an important business presentation. Then your conscious mind has the job of "turning off" the pain.

THE DIFFERENT MIND SYSTEMS

The first clue to your multifaceted mind is that your brain is made up of layers, each layer evolved at a different time in man's development.

One clue to their separate development is that each is very different in molecular structure and chemistry. Our most ancient brain is the *brain stem* which performed very well for all living creatures during millions of years of evolution in the sea. But life in the sea is relatively stable, with little temperature change and no absence of water or food. So when life crawled up on the land between 300 and 200 million years ago, a new kind of brain had to evolve.

This was the larger *limbic system* or mammalian brain that sits on top of the brain stem. No longer were we "cold as a fish." Life on land was more complex. The mammalian brain and its hypothalamus added emotion to our repertoire so we could respond in more complex ways.

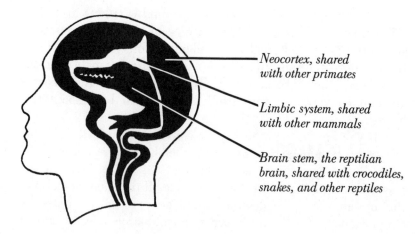

Neocortex, shared with other primates

Limbic system, shared with other mammals

Brain stem, the reptilian brain, shared with crocodiles, snakes, and other reptiles

The *cerebral cortex* appeared 50 million years ago. It made us even more adaptable, able to remember in complex ways, to speak, calculate, plan, imagine.

WHICH PART OF THE MIND IS UNDECIDED?

Can't make up your mind? Which part? Because each part of our mind considers a different aspect of an issue, it isn't surprising that we grapple with multiple opinions about things. The popular image of the mind as a giant computer is wrong. The mind is defined by renowned psychologist Howard Gardner in *Frames of Mind* and by his colleague Robert Ornstein in *Multimind: A New Way of Looking at Human Behavior* as a series of unique minds. Each newly evolved mind is linked more or less efficiently with the older minds. Together they are powerful enough to design a computer that can try to imitate the mind.

The many talents of our multipart mind are most apparent in the delightful area of language. Most five-year-olds have mastered the general syntax and idiosyncrasies of their native language, but multimillion-dollar computers remain stumped on that score. Computers have trouble recognizing misspelled words, filling in incomplete sentences, or understanding regional speech variations. Yet all of us do this at a nearly unconscious level every day, while other parts of our mind are considering the effects of the incoming information on our lives. (Computers also fail hilariously at translating one language into another.) A simple, nearly automatic human activity like getting dressed, cooking dinner, or washing the car would involve trillions of bits of information in a computer program.

THE FIVE MINDS

Imagine that the basic compartments of your mind operate something like a Board of Trustees, sitting around a conference table. At the head of the table is the Executive Mind. Flanked on each side are the other four Minds, each holding the floor in turn. Their names form an easy-to-remember acronym, WORK:

Wondering Mind
Organizing Mind
Reacting Mind
Knowing Mind

Sometimes two or more members of the board talk at once, either supporting each other or hopelessly garbling the discussion. (We are constantly arguing viewpoints and discussing compromises with ourselves.) That is when the Executive Mind steps in to settle disputes and issue orders. At the far end of the table is the recording secretary, Memory, taking the minutes of the meeting, deciding what is important enough to write down. These notes are stored in the huge bookcases that run, floor to ceiling, around the walls of the room.

Here is a brief description of five parts of the mind and their functions:

meeting of the minds

Executive Mind: Oversees, coordinates, decides, judges, gives orders, controls, enforces rules, sets priorities. For efficiency, it works from a *Manual of Procedures* that it has compiled over the years. (Can be fair, nurturing, supportive. Can also be overbearing and incite rebellion among the other members of the board.)

Wondering Mind: Explores, learns, creates, discovers, infers, experiments, is intuitive, plays. Relies on other parts of the mind for input and—usually—on the Executive Mind for permission. (Can respond mischievously with humorous or irreverent images at serious moments.)

Organizing Mind: Analyzes, sorts, crafts, orders, sequences, assembles information, is rational and logical, compares, acts on "rules" that have been established through past experience.

Reacting Mind: Experiences or supplies emotions: anger, fear, sorrow, joy, boredom, embarrassment, humor, love, compassion, psychic pain and pleasure. (Can interpret physical sensations as comfort, pain, or pleasure.)

Knowing Mind: Experiences: sees, hears, smells, tastes, has tactile and kinesthetic experiences; collects information and presents it to the other minds for processing.

THE SIXTH MIND

There is a sixth part of our mind, but since it rarely interacts with the other parts of our mind, we rarely monitor its messages. This is the functional or "silent" part of the mind. It sits quietly to one side, but it's our most important mind because it keeps us alive:

The Silent Mind: Controls all body functions: breathing, digesting, secretion, immunity, elimination, thirst, hunger, body temperature, weight regulation, growth. This part of the mind experiences direct physical sensations such as pressure, pain, pleasure. (It may be blocked from reporting these sensations accurately by orders from the other parts of the mind.)

We are generally unaware of this aspect of our mind. Yet, it can be a powerful intruder when the other parts begin to quarrel. At their instigation, it can sabotage our health, energy, and emotional well-being.

WHAT ABOUT MEMORY AND INTELLIGENCE?

You'll notice that memory is not listed among the five parts of the mind. That is because memory is a *function* of all five. Your memory could be compared to the library and record storage room of a large corporation. It records selected information from all parts of the mind, stores it, and returns it later, not always efficiently or productively, and not always as needed or requested.

The concept of intelligence is even harder to nail down. In fact, the world has yet to come up with a generally accepted definition of what it is! Most observers agree, however, that there is a difference between *capacity* and *achievement*. We all know some "smart" people who constantly spin their wheels while seemingly less-intelligent folks head straight for the finish line. A popular metaphor to explain this is cited by cognitive psychologist Roger Peters in his book, *Practical Intelligence: Working Smarter in Business and Everyday Life.*

> We each have a bucket of a size determined early
> in life, possibly at conception. Some of us have large
> buckets, but only a little knowledge sloshing
> around on the bottom. Others have smaller buckets
> that are full to the brim. And some of us
> ("geniuses") have huge buckets with lots of
> knowledge.

But Peters doesn't believe that the size of the bucket—our capacity—is really unchangeable. We'll talk about this more in chapter 12, *Staying Smart.*

First, rate yourself on how aware you have been of the separate parts of your mind.

	Very Aware	Somewhat Aware	Unaware	Want to Improve
Executive Mind (Making decisions)	☐	☐	☐	☐

	Very Aware	Somewhat Aware	Unaware	Want to Improve
Wondering Mind (Being curious)	☐	☐	☐	☐
Organizing Mind (Sorting, planning)	☐	☐	☐	☐
Reacting Mind (Responding, feeling)	☐	☐	☐	☐
Knowing Mind (Noticing, learning)	☐	☐	☐	☐

This information may help you as you discover how each element of your mind can support or sabotage the others. It is important to note that even though you may be unaware of the activities of a particular part of your mind, it can still have a strong effect on your thought processes.

Now, see if you can decide which mind skill has temporarily taken control when the following situations take place. Which other part or parts of the mind might work more effectively? (You can look at the list above to help you choose.)

	Which Part of the Mind Is in Control?	Which Part(s) Might Do a Better Job?
1. I am about to talk to my boss about something I know very well, but I get tongue-tied with embarrassment and fear that he will find something wrong.	_____	_____

	Which Part of the Mind Is in Control?	Which Part(s) Might Do a Better Job?
2. I spend most of my time dithering, being upset about things, so I don't get any real work accomplished.	_____	_____
3. I spend too much time daydreaming and can't seem to concentrate.	_____	_____
4. I'm terrified of dentists, so I rarely go.	_____	_____
5. Few people can live up to my standards.	_____	_____
6. I frequently choose friends who aren't good for me.	_____	_____
7. I sometimes get so nervous, I bite my lip until it bleeds.	_____	_____
8. Spinach is yucky!	_____	_____
9. I jump to conclusions a lot.	_____	_____
10. I often feel guilty because I don't get everything done or do it as well as I should.	_____	_____

Answers

1. Reacting   Organizing
2. Reacting   Organizing, Executive
3. Wondering   Organizing, Executive
4. Reacting   Organizing
5. Executive   Reacting
6. Reacting   Organizing
7. Reacting   Knowing
8. Reacting   Wondering
9. Wondering   Knowing
10. Executive   Wondering

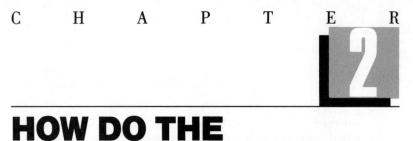

HOW DO THE
FIVE MINDS WORK?

Fred says: "I'm a procrastinator. I can never seem to
get things done when I should. Even if it's something
I enjoy doing, I put if off. People often get mad at me
because of it, and then I get disgusted with myself. I
make all kinds of promises to do better, but nothing
changes. How can I force myself to *do* things?"

Procrastination is usually a sign that the different parts of your
mind are arguing or sabotaging each other, setting up blocks. Don't
ignore these blocks—the conflict carries a message. Respect the
warning. Hang onto a block until you feel sure that you no longer
need it.

A block is a signal that on some level you believe that doing
what you are "supposed" to do might be harmful, or that not doing it
might be beneficial. Some blocks are destructive, signs of a serious
problem that may require professional help. Many, however, are
garden-variety, everyday nuisance blocks that can be overcome by
monitoring the conversations taking place between the parts of
your mind.

"What thing do you procrastinate about that concerns you
most?" I asked Fred.

"The thing that gets me in the most trouble is that I can't seem to sit down and pay the bills. I have enough money in my checking account, but I just don't get to it. Once they even shut off the phone because I was late with the check."

Fred readily acknowledged that extreme poverty in his child-hood probably made him very cautious with his money. Now he had achieved a degree of financial comfort, but he still had a fear of being poor and helpless again, a fear he combated irrationally by putting off paying his bills. He recognized how ridiculous this was, but he continued to procrastinate until the problem became a major irritant. Now he was ready to change his behavior. Instead of probing deep into his childhood memories, I suggested that we listen in on the different parts of his mind as they discussed the problem.

"Tell me about paying bills, Fred," I said.

"You have to pay bills on time!"

"Which part of your mind is saying that?"

"The executive part, I guess. It's what I keep telling myself."

"And . . . ?" I continued.

"You get in trouble if you don't pay bills on time."

"Is that the reacting part of your mind talking? Are you responding emotionally? Or is it analytical . . . the organizing part talking?"

" . . . Organizing, I guess. My credit rating gets messed up. I lose more in penalty payments than I get in extra interest."

"What else?" I asked. He looked blank. So I asked him to reconstruct where he sat and how he acted when he paid bills. Sometimes this triggers valuable clues to disruptive blocks, but not this time. Fred reported no discomfort with the physical process itself.

"Where do you keep your bills before they're paid?" I asked. Fred seemed uneasy and shifted in his seat. "Fred, try to form a strong mental picture of picking up the mail and finding a bill. What happens then? Describe it."

"Oh, sometimes I put them on the hall table, sometimes on my desk, sometimes by the phone in the kitchen. No regular place." (The noticing part of his mind may be responding to messages from one or more of the other parts: "Don't notice.")

"I notice that you are very observant of many things in your personal and professional life," I told Fred. "Why do you think you don't notice something like where you put the bills?"

"I don't want to know," Fred said, smiling ruefully. "I told you. That's my block."

Fred readily agreed that emotionally he was setting himself up for conflict by constantly reminding himself about times when he felt powerless because he had no money. He described several such occasions, but acknowledged that the small amounts of money he hangs on to by not paying his phone or gas bill would not prevent future helplessness. Ironically this block actually promotes helplessness. But understanding why we do something and changing the way we do it are still a crucial step apart.

We discussed getting Fred's sense of wonder and curiosity to look for a new way to view bill paying. The wondering part of the mind loves playing games, so I suggested that Fred play out a scene in which he is standing in his home on a Saturday morning while his various minds give him instructions about paying the bills. Self-consciously at first, Fred went through the messages that each part of his mind had been presenting:

meeting of the minds

Executive Part: "You must pay my bills on time!"

Organizing Part: "You lose more in penalty payments than you get in extra interest when you pay late."

Reacting Part: "What if you're caught with no money at all? Remember the humiliation, the fear, the powerlessness! Hang on to every penny!"

Organizing Part: "That's completely illogical."

Reacting Part: "I know, but I don't care!"

Knowing Part: "While you guys are arguing, I refuse to notice where the bills are. You don't want to pay them anyway."

Wondering Part: "What great opportunities for my creative efforts! Imagine having the electricity shut off: Oh, my God! The World Series and no television! Oh! Oh! Or you're sleeping in the gutter. And while you picture all that, what if I put some cash in a safe place in the house, enough to cover an emergency? Then will you feel safe? Then will you pay the bills?"

Reacting Part: "What if the house burns down?"

Wondering Part: "I'll hide the money in silver dollars. They won't burn."

Reacting Part: "Well . . . okay." (*in a smug voice*) "Then I won't worry any more."

And Fred collapsed into a chair, entertained but drained by his vigorous playacting. It looked as though we had made a breakthrough.

Unfortunately not all such sessions have the desired long-term effect. The client enjoys the stimulation of the discovery, but doesn't put it to use. The old ways, even painful ones, are just too comfortable and reassuring.

So several months later I checked back with Fred. He reported that he now sat down every Saturday morning and wrote checks for household expenses. When he didn't feel like it, he would replay the scene in my office in which the different parts of his mind argued among themselves. It rarely took more than a few exchanges before he felt ready to report to his desk and reach for his checkbook.

"What about hiding money in the house?" I asked. "Did you do that?"

"Well, I thought about it seriously, but it didn't seem practical. So I got one of those silver dollar paperweights and I put all the bills under it as they come in the mail."

Just like five executives around a boardroom conference table, each part of your mind has a different agenda, a different set of priorities and values.

meeting of the minds

Wondering Part: Novelty, change, something new—wants to play.

Organizing Part: Familiar patterns, identifiable structures—wants to evaluate.

Reacting Part: Ideal level of stimulation (which fluctuates)—wants to respond.

Knowing Part: Intellectual exercise, stimulation of the senses, absence of extreme discomfort—wants to be stimulated.

Executive Part: Power, ego-fulfillment—wants to control.

Is it any wonder that sometimes we don't know our own mind? Let's take a closer look at the roles that the different parts of the mind play in our daily lives.

THE EXECUTIVE PART

Mona takes a little longer than most people to make up her mind. She weighs the alternatives, even writes down lists of pros and cons. Her husband, Harry, sometimes teases her about her cautious approach to life, but once Mona has made up her mind, she wastes no energy wondering if she made the right choice. ("After all, that's how I decided to marry *you*, dear," she reminds him, smiling. "I listed all the advantages and disadvantages and you won.") Whatever the outcome of Mona's decision, she never torments herself by playing "what if" or "if only." Her Executive Mind is a good manager.

The executive part of the mind is like a Chairman of the Board. It tries to control, coordinate, and maintain harmony. Like many executives, it doesn't always know what the other parts are up to, and it can be outvoted at times.

The executive part can consider a variety of actions and reactions. At the local level, the information processing of a rubbing shoe has no alternative: it makes a blister. At the executive level, the mind starts a conversation, checking the blister against its acquired *Manual of Procedures* which provides information and alternatives for action.

Much of the mind's background information is stored in a *Manual of Procedures.* Everything you think and experience has a chance of making it into this unique file that makes up your personality, beliefs, and philosophy of life.

Like every corporate *Manual of Procedures,* this policy file can contain outdated, contradictory, or erroneous information. If the manual becomes too convoluted, the mind might make wildly irrational decisions or become nearly immobilized.

Fortunately, choice and freedom are also human activities. Through the executive part of the mind we can observe ourselves as we create our own beliefs.

To understand how our mind can form ideas and abstractions, imagine walking through a fun house that has spinning floors, tilting walls, and mirrors everywhere that add to the confusion. You do something and then watch the result. Then your mind can judge what the action has accomplished and whether to alter it in the future. You *must* have feedback before you can begin to decide on a "right" and a "wrong." Ultimately you build up a data base so that many complex tasks and decisions become nearly automatic.

Of course, consistently faulty reporting by one part of the mind can influence faulty decision making at the top. The people who turn off messages like "That's dangerous!" or "That's wrong!" because "I was told to do it" or "Everyone else is doing it" or even "It might be fun!" are giving themselves flawed input for decision making.

People who have superbly developed organizing and wondering skills but defective reacting abilities may easily convince their Executive Minds that it is okay to commit atrocities in the name of science. People who have developed extreme sensitivity to their own reactions may be very aware of their own needs and responses, but never observe and report the effects that their impulsive actions have on others. People with undeveloped organizational skills may note only the few details that fill their own simplistic interpretation of reality. They are closed to new information.

On the other hand, a strong executive part that demands subservience from all the other aspects of the mind is in trouble. Even if we *could* live up to an ideal of behavior and beliefs manufactured by our executive part, it would be self-defeating. The incredible variety of input we process is constantly forming a new reality and a new ideal. An autocratic executive with ironclad rules and values would shut down the mind to all but the most primitive and basic information processing. The executive part of the mind needs to be a kindly and wise overseer, flexible, perceptive, even somewhat ingenuous in accepting all input before handing down decisions.

Lily Tomlin's character, Trudy the Bag Lady, says, "Reality is just a collective hunch." Our reality is made up of the collective hunches of the four branch-manager parts of our mind, interpreted and modified by the executive part.

THE WONDERING MIND

One of my easiest but most intriguing cases was with film critic Sheila Benson. She had begun her career writing reviews for the *Pacific Sun*, a northern California newspaper. Her breezy style and on-target perceptions soon brought her a job offer from the larger *Los Angeles Times* at a lot more money. But her exhilaration quickly soured: "After I got here, I began to be worried that they needed some godlike person (who wasn't me) to dispense information. The *Pacific Sun* was on a scale I could understand while this new place was vast and a little overwhelming. I began to tighten up in the writing and the deadline schedule began to spook me." The critical executive part of her mind was sabotaging her creativity by saying "This is *important*—do better!"

"Tell me what it was like when you wrote for the *Pacific Sun*," I said.

"Oh, that was lots of fun. It was like writing for friends."

I suggested that she go back and visualize the point where her work was fun and manageable. "It's the you that writes for the *Pacific Sun* that they hired," I pointed out. She realized this and got the critical part of her mind to leave the creative part alone.

The wondering part of the mind is creative, eager to learn, intuitive and childlike. It is the part of us that puts pieces together into wholes, that infers wholes from fragmented parts, and that seeks out new information for our other minds to respond to. The knowing part may spot something it hasn't encountered before, but it is the curious wondering part that lets us decide to stop and really notice it, to supply meaning to it, and to pass that information along to the analytical organizing part for processing.

THE ORGANIZING MIND

If you were presented with a list of a hundred random objects and asked to organize the information, you could probably think of a dozen or more ways to do it: alphabetically, animate and inanimate, larger or smaller than a bread box, tangible and intangible, manufactured or existing in nature, by cost, by desirability, by estimated weight, by number of legs or wheels, by degree of mobility, by "goodness" or "badness," and so forth. To do this, you would use your inborn organizing ability, relatively unhampered by the other parts of your mind (unless you were hungry or tired).

The organizing part of your mind is your problem solver. It puts information together in rational sequences. It compares one thing to another, evaluates, chooses among, and discards from the millions of bits of information that assault us every hour. It makes these decisions using information supplied to it by the rest of the mind. It is the part of you that is constantly judging how well you are doing— sometimes when you don't want it to.

This is the voice that tells you: "Smoking causes cancer." "Be an informed voter." "Don't borrow at current interest rates." One or more of the other parts of your mind may overrule it, and then you have a contradiction between your actions and your beliefs.

The most common conflict comes when your matter-of-fact organizing ability and your emotional reactions clash. In our model of the boardroom conference table, we would have to put organizing ability and emotional reaction on either side of the executive chairman. They are the two parts that *must* work in unison for us to be truly productive.

THE REACTING MIND

Harvey was terrified of cats. Whenever he'd see one, even in a magazine ad, his heart would pound, he'd break out in a sweat, his stomach would churn, and sometimes he'd be close to passing out. He had tried to hide this "weakness" for years, but more and more it took over his life until he was restricted in where he could live, work, and shop, and with whom he could socialize. When we sat down together, he had decided that something had to change.

Some analysts might wander through Harvey's psyche for years, trying to find the root of this fascinating phobia. I have found "Redecision Therapy" to be much quicker and often more effective. In that system, developed by Mary Goulding and Robert Goulding, M.D., the patient "re-decides" in one session to change something in his life. Their book, *Changing Lives through Redecision Therapy,* urges readers not to "work on it" or "talk about it," but to *change* it.

So Harvey began describing what happened when he so much as thought about a cat, ". . . and I make myself sick." This is the key of our emotions: we provide emotional responses on cue. The cue may be elementary—a sudden fall or a scratch on your back where it itches. The fear or pleasure response is automatic. But knowledge of special circumstances can reverse the responses or eliminate them: suppose we fall down a flight of stairs in a burning building and land close to safety at the front door; what if the scratch on the back comes when we think we are totally alone; or perhaps falls or back scratches are such common occurrences for us that we stop noticing them.

The situation is an *occasion* for emotional response. We decide what kind of response it will be. In Harvey's case, his reacting mind furnished an emotional response the organizing and executive parts didn't want. He finally persuaded himself to respond differently. Through skillful negotiation, he persuaded himself that his response was obsolete and could be comfortably replaced by another response.

Did it work? Harvey isn't raising prize Persians yet, but he can handle an occasional encounter with a cat more easily. He has broadened his world to include places where cats may be; and each time he meets one and chooses *not* to be afraid, his new response pattern is strengthened.

We have always known that different people react with different emotional intensity to similar stimuli. Some people burst into tears if they are caught in a sudden spring shower, while others deal calmly with an actual flood. Recent studies by psychologists at Purdue University indicate that our degree of emotional intensity —the tendency to amplify or diminish reactions—appears quite early in life. As reported in *Developmental Psychology,* the Purdue researchers asked the parents of 76 college students to describe those same students as children—how fussy or tranquil they had been. They found that the parents' ratings corresponded closely with separate evaluations of the students' emotional intensity as young adults.

Fortunately for fussy babies, another 1986 study reported that they mellow with age. An evaluation of 242 people aged 15 to 70 found that intense emotional reactions decrease each decade of life. The biggest change comes between the ages of 20 and 40. So there is some justification for the saying, "Grow up!"

Highly reactive people tend to be less sophisticated, according to a recent study by Yale/Chicago Medical College researchers, and, ironically, they are less aware of their own emotions! But despite the more pronounced highs and lows of their own emotions, the highly reactive subjects reported the same degree of contentment with their lives as did those whose lives were free of this self-produced turmoil. Quite possibly, highly reactive people need a high level of stimulation to function, so they create it within themselves.

This doesn't mean that we should try to lower our emotional responses. The knowing part of our mind notices, but our emotions *recognize*. It is absolutely essential to have a healthy, active Reacting Mind to be a healthy, active person. The Reacting Mind must work vigorously with the other parts of our minds to supply much of life's meaning. Sometimes internal or external messages try to destroy the balance of the various mind elements, suppressing one in favor of another. The Reacting Mind is a frequent target of outside messages: "Don't be a crybaby." "We Joneses have terrible tempers." "Those guys are always out to get you." "All the men in our family have been heroes." These messages get considered and recorded in our *Manual of Procedures*.

Our ability to supply the "correct" emotion is affected by such messages. Outside events or internal sensations and thoughts can suggest an emotional response, but that response isn't inevitable. We can control our emotions just as we can control our other mind processes. We will discuss how to "cue" these responses in chapter 13.

THE KNOWING MIND

Janie is in the middle of discussing a business deal with an important out-of-town buyer when she decides that she is not making an impression. She alters her approach to one that worked with a similar client and makes the sale.

Paul is looking at used cars. He walks around the lot, thumping this one and patting that one. Finally a blue one catches his eye, the same delightful shade of blue as the car his parents owned when he was a child. He has happy memories of whizzing along sunny country roads in that car. Paul opens the car door and an exciting odor overwhelms him, the distinctive aroma of a fine, new car. This, he decides, is it!

Stephanie coordinates her wardrobe to her energy level. On days when she is feeling overloaded, she tends to wear quiet, neutral colors. When she is either very cheerful or slightly depressed, she wears bright colors. On days when she is at low ebb, she chooses dark colors, but with a touch of bright. During the day she focuses occasionally on the bright scarf or bracelet, using the classic psychological principle: Acknowledge where you are and then move to where you want to be. Although many people find blue and green very soothing, she thinks they're both "depressing—I never wear them." Stephanie consciously uses her response to colors to support and improve her mental abilities.

The knowing part of the mind is different from the other four because its skills occupy identifiable areas of the brain. There are specific locations for recording sights, sounds, smells, and tastes. Unlike a camera or tape recorder, the Knowing Mind compares much of its intake with that of the other minds to see what information should be sought out and passed along. Its intake can be colored by emotions, giving neutral information a powerful shading of drama. It can also be limited when the organizing part lets us know in advance what to look for, creating an efficient but restrictive kind of tunnel vision.

The knowing part is also strongly affected by emotional "scripts" and by injunctions from the *Manual of Procedures*. If we write a script that says that automobiles or movie stars are fascinating, we quickly learn to tell a Ford from a Plymouth, or Paul Newman from Robert Redford. An injunction from our inner executive (perhaps voiced by Mother) says, "It's not polite to notice that," and so we turn off our previously keen observation of handicapped people or of Uncle Charlie's drunken sprees or of the physical differences between boys and girls.

THE SILENT MIND

Whenever Tracy was depressed about her life, she automatically got a cold or broke out in cold sores. When Glenn was under pressure at work, he forgot to eat. Henry sometimes was so engrossed in his work that he would literally forget to breathe for brief periods. Then he'd get a headache from lack of oxygen.

In each case, messages from the basic survival system were being ignored or blocked by the babble of general internal conversations.

Much of the work of the silent part of the mind is below our level of conscious thought most of the time: processes like breathing, digesting, healing, immunity, handling waste, body temperature control, and growth. Some functions pop up to awareness level periodically: thirst, hunger, cold, the need to go to the bathroom. Of course, sexual arousal is a complex conversation between several of our minds.

Other responses are subtly manipulated by advertisers, friends, and medical professionals. Knowledgeable nurses pop bedpans under patients, turn on the tap in the hospital room sink, and leave the room. They know that people tend to have a certain functional response to the sound of running water.

Of course, we can focus on many of our automatic functions and control them. You can change your rate of breathing, or think about your next meal and notice how your salivary glands respond. There are even some highly trained and motivated individuals who can control their pulse, oxygen consumption, body temperature, and metabolic rate with their conscious minds.

The Silent Mind recognizes all the physical sensations we are experiencing and decides whether or not to notify the rest of the mind about its findings. Much of what the Silent Mind notices is below our level of consciousness. Think of it as a quiet bookkeeper, toiling away in the background and notifying others only when data is requested or when a disaster is imminent. It also uses pain to make you aware of major and minor physical changes in your surroundings and within yourself.

As quiet as it is, our Silent Mind plays a powerful role in keeping the mind on track. It can distract blatantly or subtly. It can support orderly progress by helping us to feel comfortable and centered. It can also be tricked by the other minds into giving erroneous information.

How aware are you of the executive functions of your mind? Here are some value calls that you frequently make. (There are no right or wrong answers.)

	Strongly Agree/ Always 5	Often 4	No Opinion/ Sometimes 3	Rarely 2	Strongly Disagree/ Never 1
I give money to pan- handlers.	5	4	3	2	1
I lend money to friends.	5	4	3	2	1
I throw candy and cigarette wrappers on the ground.	5	4	3	2	1

	Strongly Agree/ Always	Often	No Opinion/ Sometimes	Rarely	Strongly Disagree/ Never
	5	**4**	**3**	**2**	**1**
A good education is the most important thing for a child.	5	4	3	2	1
I will sacrifice in other areas to own a new car.	5	4	3	2	1
My career comes first right now.	5	4	3	2	1
One cannot be a good person without religion.	5	4	3	2	1
I can't stand overweight people.	5	4	3	2	1
Health is more important than wealth.	5	4	3	2	1
I cheat on my income tax.	5	4	3	2	1
I visit the dentist regularly.	5	4	3	2	1
I'd do almost anything to help a good friend.	5	4	3	2	1

	Strongly Agree/ Always **5**	Often **4**	No Opinion/ Sometimes **3**	Rarely **2**	Strongly Disagree/ Never **1**
I'd choose a high-paying, boring job over an interesting but low-paying one.	5	4	3	2	1
I'm too independent and set in my ways to live with anyone.	5	4	3	2	1
Even if a low-rent housing development would endanger a species of butterfly, I'd vote for building the houses. People are more important than butterflies.	5	4	3	2	1
God doesn't exist.	5	4	3	2	1
I'd die for my country.	5	4	3	2	1

Whatever your answers, they represent decisions you have made after weighing the input of the different parts of your mind. The fascinating thing about your mind is that it will be called upon to make some of these decisions over and over throughout your lifetime—not *every* decision, because that would be unproductive and exhausting. But many things change. The feedback of each part of your mind constantly provides new information. The world of your reality will change, both internally and externally. You will alter decisions to accommodate the change.

When all parts of your mind work together smoothly, you are capable of almost anything! What would you like to do differently in your life? Write it down:

Right now I _____.
Instead, I will _____.

What do the parts of your mind say about this?

Executive _____

This is probably a statement about something you should change. It is based on data accumulated in your *Manual of Procedures* plus any new input processed by your organizing system ("Your blood pressure is too high." "The stock market went down today.") Do the other parts of your mind agree? Let's check them out. First, imagine the change has happened. What does the logical organizing part of your mind say?

Organizing _____

Any conflicts so far? Go on to your emotional reaction and look for any responses that may disagree.

Reacting _____

How do the previous conversations fit in with what you know about your goal?

Knowing _____

Now the wondering part of your mind should have a lot of data to work with. What solutions, compromises, breakthroughs can it suggest? Don't be afraid to make some outrageously silly proposals. Be playful!

Wondering _____

Have you found a key to change that satisfies the needs of each part of your mind? Just ordering change rarely works (as every parent knows!). You have to enlist each part of your mind with its unique and appropriate talents to respond to the new plan. Like a successful manager, the executive part sets a goal and then gets the cooperation of all the board members, devising ways to excite their individual enthusiasm and support.

OVERCOMING
BLOCKS

David, a Harvard graduate, came to me about a "simple writing block." He was now a professor at an eastern university and needed to finish a book to gain promotion and tenure. The deadline was so pressing that he had isolated himself from his family, working in a basement room each weekend.

We explored and eliminated several of the common causes of writing blocks. I even checked out whether this self-imposed isolation might not be a way of avoiding or punishing his family, but this didn't seem to be the case either.

Then I asked him where he used to study as a kid. He remembered his father making him do his homework on a back porch, isolated from the rest of his family. I asked him to imagine himself as that younger David writing on the back porch.

"How do you feel?" I asked.

"Anxious," he replied. "Eventually my father will visit, look over what I've done, and criticize my work."

"How do you feel in your basement room?"

A smile of recognition broke out. "Anxious! Just like I used to feel on the back porch."

David agreed to imagine himself as his father Matthew and let me interview him.

"Matthew, what kind of son was David?"

"Very bright—he used to scare me. I was afraid he'd get to be smarter than me."

"Matthew, imagine that David has written his book, has had it published, that it has attracted rave reviews, has gotten him his promotion, and that you have read it. What is your reaction?"

"I'm jealous. A little scared. I'm jealous because I had to quit school after the fourth grade to work the farm. I've never had the chances David had. I was always afraid that if David got smarter he wouldn't talk with me and he'd be ashamed. I tried to keep him down by looking for mistakes and acting like he wasn't so smart."

David discovered that, as a result of working with unproven or outdated information, he had been preventing himself from succeeding in order to "protect" his father. He now recognized the situation and was free to find ways to remain close to his father that didn't require David to hide his capability. Succeeding at his job no longer put his love for his father in jeopardy.

Mental blocks are important. They're like warning flags, saying "Look out!" Blocks are a valuable protective device, thrown up by one or more parts of the mind for our own good. Don't ever give up a block until you are sure that you don't need it any more.

Most mental blocks occur when the various elements of the mind are at cross purposes or when one part of the mind fails to make accurate reports to the others. Much of my private therapy work is with people who have blocks—writing blocks, memory blocks, speaking-in-public blocks, success blocks, intimacy blocks. These people come to a point where they will try almost anything to overcome the block.

Author Joyce Carol Oates has a superb description of writer's block, but I think it applies to most blocks: ". . . a temporary paralysis of the imagination caused by the conviction, on an unconscious level, that what the [person] is attempting is in some way fraudulent, or mistaken, or self-destructive."

But what part of your mind is telling you that you are mistaken? What part fears destruction? And is that assessment accurate? By discovering which part of your mind is producing the conflict, you will be able to put the issue before the full Board of Directors to evaluate and resolve.

Myrna was assigned to approach the predominantly male department heads at her firm with the message from the top: "Hire more women." Although she firmly believed in this policy, she still found herself paralyzed with fear when she began her presentations, stuttering and generally making a fool of herself. "How can I persuade them that women will do a great job when I look incompetent myself?" she asked me.

She was a confident, articulate person. It was hard to imagine her tongue-tied. I asked her to pretend that I was a department head and persuade me. She delivered a very convincing presentation.

Then I asked her to imagine she was in the office of one of the men with whom she felt uncomfortable. Immediately she began to freeze up. "What's different this time?" I asked. After exploring several possibilities, Myrna decided that these disapproving older men reminded her of her father and his constant complaints about her career: "You're 28 years old and you're not married!"

Myrna had used her organizational ability to prepare some very persuasive arguments for her presentations, but her emotional reaction was one of overwhelming feelings of inadequacy and failure: "No one will love you."

Knowing the cause of a problem doesn't automatically eliminate it. She admitted she knew perfectly well that she had other sources of love besides these business associates. "Do you believe that confronting people on business issues is risky?" I asked. "Does it make them respect you less?" She decided that she confronted people every day and that usually they probably respected her more. She recognized that she was taking her reaction to her father's criticism and reproducing it automatically in response to the real or imagined disapproval of her male coworkers. Her father and her coworkers were different people and her reaction did not have to be the same.

"How would you like to feel when you approach these men?" I asked. We practiced a technique that I find very helpful for any high-stress situation: experiencing the natural adrenaline rush as energy for the task, rather than crippling fear.

A classic experiment reported in *Psychological Review* shows how being aware of our body's response to adrenaline affects behavior. Volunteers were given adrenaline. Some were told it was a medication that might improve their vision. The others were told it was adrenaline and would stimulate them. Then all were given a written test which contained some insulting personal questions. During the test period, a planted "stooge" crumpled up his test paper and stormed out in mock disgust. The volunteers who thought they had received an eye medication responded to the stooge's angry behavior and reported that the questionnaire had made them angry. The subjects who knew they had received adrenaline reported experiencing no particular emotion. Conclusion: *Knowing* that your body is experiencing a rush of adrenaline allows you to *choose* your response.

Stella arrived at my office, anxious to solve a writing block she had with her doctoral dissertation. Despite her enthusiasm for her subject, she resisted sitting down to do the necessary writing. Again we explored the usual reasons for writing blocks, but they didn't seem to apply. Then I asked her what was supposed to happen after she finished her doctorate.

"I promised my husband I'd have a baby."

"Do you want a baby?" I asked.

She seemed startled. Not want a baby? There was a long silence before she blurted out, "I *don't* want to have a baby!"

Stella's entire upbringing had been focused on marrying and having a family. When she got married in graduate school, her husband had agreed to postpone children until she got her degree. By not writing her dissertation, she bought time and an excuse to postpone confronting this all important issue—a truly innovative form of birth control! Our work together moved her toward deciding that creating a dissertation and creating a child were separate issues. She was able to free herself from the hidden sabotage of her emotions.

Ralph had already decided that the reason he kept hurting himself—getting into fights, being injured in frequent accidents, doing outrageous things that got him in trouble—was because his parents had both been alcoholics. Even though they were both dead, he was still trying to get their attention.

Richard Bandler, co-creator of neuro-linguistic programming, writes in *Using Your Brain—for a Change:*

> Some people will look you straight in the eye and tell you the reason they are the way they are is because of

something that happened long ago in their childhood.
If that's true, they are really stuck, because of course
then nothing can be done about it; you can't go
have your childhood again.

Fortunately, Bandler believes that you can *reframe* any experience.
People do this constantly (usually unconsciously), turning themselves into the victor, the victim, key player, or innocent bystander
of everyday occurrences—any role that makes them comfortable.
Healthy people always see themselves as *slightly* better than others
see them, more attractive, smarter, more competent. Both individuals and governments are constantly rewriting history for their own
benefit. Why then, with this powerful instinct for comforting self-
deception, do some people choose to frame a past event to make
themselves miserable, frightened, guilt-ridden, angry, or depressed?

Some of us, psychiatrist Robert Goulding has written, choose
to get locked into a negative behavior because we believe: "If I feel
bad enough long enough, I can change someone in my past." This is
a magical belief: "If I'm miserable long enough, Mom or Dad will
rescue me." If you are stuck in this system, try reframing your
negative emotional responses into realistically positive ones. Start
by answering some questions:

How do my bad feelings help me? _____

How do they hurt me? _____

Am I ready to choose to feel a different way? _____

If I choose to change my feelings, the negative emotion
I'm going to give up is _____

From now on, when I start to feel _____

I'll switch to _____

As children we had to make generalizations about the world
from incomplete data. As healthy adults, we react to what's happening now, rather than projecting bad feelings from the past onto
situations in the present.

On the following page are some common blocks. Notice the
clues they offer to which parts of the mind are in conflict:

The Block	Possible Source	Possible Solution
"I'm terrified of speaking in public. I get tongue-tied and break out in a sweat."	Silent mind system is stimulating adrenaline rush in response to situation. You choose to experience this sensation as *fear.*	Executive part issues new order: This sensation now means *excitement and energy* for the task.
"I forget people's names in important business situations."	You focus on uncomfortable sensations, blocking memory.	Your curiosity needs to take charge: "*Who* is that?!"
"I'm supposed to have a yearly medical test, but I can never bring myself to do it."	You fear bad news. Your natural curiosity is sabotaged into turning off its eagerness to learn results. ("No news is good news.")	Your mental executive notices, alerts mind to discomfort and energy expenditure, offers to nurture you through any crisis and diverts you by helping to create vivid pictures of powerful, positive feelings after the test. (Promises to take charge if news is bad.)

The Block	Possible Source	Possible Solution
"When I look at my checkbook, my mind turns to mush. I panic and can't add 5 and 8, so I'm always bouncing checks."	Emotional reaction is preprogrammed anxiety response.	Mental executive asks your playful mind to devise ten strategies for solving problem: 1. Close checking account; 2. Use calculator; 3. Use colored pencils; 4. Devise extravagant but cost-free rewards for yourself whenever your balance agrees with bank statement; etc., etc. (Could also explore origin of anxiety, but play may be quicker and just as effective.)
"I think vaguely about eating better and exercising more, but something always seems to prevent me from doing so."	You are choosing (correctly) a present physical pleasure over an uncertain and intellectualized distant future pleasure.	Your executive plots to unite all parts of the mind on a course of action: imagination creates picture of future pleasure so strong that emotions can experience it *now.* You organize ways to provide maximum sensory input and immediate rewards.

Sometimes we are at such cross purposes that we end up sabotaging ourselves. Two or more parts of the mind are in conflict and an executive decision is needed. Which parts of the mind do you think are disagreeing in the following situations?

1. I have trouble
   setting goals.   _____ and _____

2. I can't make up my
   mind about moving/
   getting married/
   starting my own
   business.   _____ and _____

3. I'm often too shy at
   parties.   _____ and _____

4. I should quit smok-
   ing, but I just can't.   _____ and _____

5. I'd love to go back
   to school, but I'd be
   too embarrassed.   _____ and _____

6. Learning new things
   is hard for me.   _____ and _____

7. Stress gives me a
   headache/heartburn/
   hives.   _____ and _____

Answers

1. Organizing and Reacting (analytic and emotional)
2. Organizing and Reacting (analytic and emotional)
3. Knowing and Reacting (noticing others and noticing self)
4. Knowing and Executive (immediate physical pleasure and decision for long-term good)
5. Wondering and Reacting (curiosity and emotions)
6. Wondering and Executive (natural curiosity and negative skill evaluation)
7. Reacting and Silent (emotions and immune system)

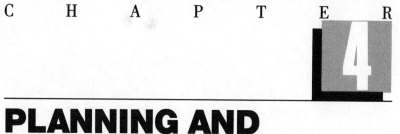

PLANNING AND PRIORITIZING

Jerry says: "I have trouble making decisions—
about changing jobs, going back to school, buying a
house, even getting my hair cut."

When you have trouble making decisions, your mental executive is getting mixed signals from the other parts of your mind. Frequently the somewhat impersonal organizing part is in conflict with your emotions; you see the advantages of a course of action, but it feels uncomfortable and threatening. This sets up a pattern, like a parent saying "You must!" and a child saying "I will not!" If the emotional part of your mind gets stuck in this rebellious role— decides to cast itself as the town troublemaker—it can make a career of producing mental blocks.

Here's some important news: healthy emotions are not childish and immature. The emotional part of your mind is capable of grandeur, altruism, infinite poetry. Don't try to block emotional messages because you think they will make you "weak." Respect and encourage the input of your emotions. Treat them as "adult" and they will respond with the support you need for your most difficult tasks.

SELECTIVE FORGETTING

Putting tasks in a logical sequence is one of the main jobs of the mind. This is a skill routinely taught in school. Some tasks fall comfortably and logically into a sequence. Others present a real challenge to order, like pursuing a broken string of pearls on a storm-tossed ship. Where do you start? How do you keep from losing one? Which pearl do you go for first? What if you forget one?

Astonishingly, forgetting can actually *help* you to plan on a large scale and set priorities. When you have too many or conflicting "to do's," you need Selective Forgetting. Start by making a list of the options. Then do something else that is *totally* engrossing: play a video game, work a crossword puzzle, skydive. When you finish this diversion, mentally go back over your "to do" list and jot down the ones you remember.

Now look at each item and decide which part or parts of your mind found that one important enough to file in memory. These are the actions that should get your first consideration. You may decide to overrule some of them, but that becomes a *conscious* decision on your part. You will be far less likely to have one part of your mind quietly sabotaging the others to get its pet project put through.

Selective Forgetting also alerts you to review the original list and fill in the unexciting "must do's." Seen in the context of the larger plan which *you* have designed and *you* control, these niggling details won't be as arduous.

WHY PLAN?

Some people maintain that planning takes the fun and spontaneity out of life. These folks are usually fond of quoting (often incorrectly) Matthew 6:34:

> Take therefore no thought for the morrow: for
> the morrow shall take thought for the things of itself.
> Sufficient unto the day is the evil thereof.

Biblical scholars can debate the exact meaning of this passage, but I prefer to think that it asks us not to regard today's pain as permanent and eternal. When we are drowning in troubles, a popular coping technique is to live "a day at a time." This is a good way to deal with an overwhelmingly large problem—divide it up into small, bite-sized chunks. But even this approach requires *planning*. Which chunk first? In what order? At what rate? And without plans for the *good* stuff in life, we are left with only an obsession for the "evil" of the day.

People who have no plans—flexible, short-range, long-range, and contingency plans always open to the excitement of serendipity —are like jellyfish drifting with the tide. For the jellyfish, life consists of drifting back and forth between existence in the water and extinction on the shore. Farther out in the ocean are the whales and dolphins, cavorting, playing, enjoying themselves immensely, but always following their migration patterns, their *plans*. Is the life plan of a whale really more restrictive than the drifting of a jellyfish?

Far from overwhelming us, long-term plans make temporary setbacks more bearable by showing what a small role they play in the larger picture. Conscious long-term planning is a feature that we like to think is unique to the human mind. If we have this incredible gift, shouldn't we use it? Anyone without a variety of plans is no better off than a jellyfish, vulnerable to a casual eddy that might send it to its doom on the shore.

Making plans is an executive function. Your organizational skill can provide much of the data necessary to prepare and carry out the plan. The knowing and emotional parts of your mind will, if consulted, list their requirements for optimum well-being and state what they can contribute. Your creativity can devise new strategies for reaching a particular goal. But ultimately the executive part of the mind must form the plans.

Mid-range and long-range plans should be as realistic as possible and deserve some extensive board meetings of the mind. Too grandiose and they are doomed to failure; too mundane and they doom *you* to failure. That is a failure of the spirit and of the potential of your magnificent, many-talented mind.

MAKING A LIFE PLAN

Anatole France commented: "We do not know what to do with this short life, yet we yearn for another that will be eternal."

What is your life plan and how did you devise it? Many people read books and attend seminars, half expecting to encounter a revelation, a sudden insight or spark that will change their perspective on the world in positive ways. Recently a friend of mine attended a workshop and returned home proclaiming that her entire life had changed. The intriguing thing is that this wasn't a seminar on spiritual growth or self-awareness or even a religious retreat. It was a quilt design workshop conducted by a nationally known quilt designer, Nancy Crow. My friend's story illustrates a change on the level of the Executive Mind that sets policy for all the other minds.

> She said: "Needlework has always seemed to be the natural and required pastime of women, not an art form worthy of support and comment. Therefore, I was stunned and thrilled to find myself in an environment where time spent on creating was not regarded as time taken away from 'important' things.
> We were told 'Don't give anything away.' (I have made and given away more than a hundred quilts, sweaters, rugs, and garments—doesn't a person give best who gives of herself?) 'No,' Ms. Crow said firmly. 'No one truly values what is free. Don't even sell your work unless you have to. You must acquire a *Body of Work*.' "

This "Body of Work" concept has been resonating in my mind ever since. Almost everything we do should and can become part of our Body of Work. Once we have designed our life, the most mundane activity that supports that design is a contribution to our legacy.

The homemaker whose conscious life plan is to create a warm, healthy, safe, and stimulating home can then see the boring tasks of mending or scrubbing as an essential part of the greater design. She can also understand that time for reading, study, or creativity is not time taken away from her main purpose but an addition to it.

The brain surgeon who wants to conquer death and pain is able to interpret reading a comic book or cleaning the basement as essential to maintaining his equilibrium. The executive who is getting ulcers over poor sales has to balance this setback with his success at checkers and in caring for his aged mother. The recently divorced person must see the achievements in still paying household bills on time and remembering to put out the garbage on the right night.

The person who sees his low-man-on-the-totem-pole job as a rung on a lofty ladder to success can perform the most menial tasks without disdain because they are background in a larger canvas. And the person who must take an unfulfilling job to support a family can keep a healthier mental balance if he sees this labor as part of a greater design, the survival and growth of his children.

A Body of Work does not have to be a concrete pile of books or paintings or a record of building buildings or founding foundations. It can be as abstract as creating enduring enthusiasm among others for Arizona cacti or Texas chile or the works of Herman Melville, because of your knowledge. This legacy of mentorship can have limitless influence on generations to come.

Viewing your life as a legacy brings astonishing liberation along with awesome responsibilities. Suddenly you are no longer free just to bounce along, taking what comes. Without giving up the glorious freedom of daily choices and redefinitions, you must see your life through the small end of the telescope—few details but a strong outline.

The details get filled in as you go, and, knowing the larger plan, you are better able to choose what you want to do. Imagine pushing a shopping cart through a supermarket without knowing whether you are shopping for a Thanksgiving dinner or a Fourth of July picnic. You can compare having a life plan to deciding what kind of meal you are going to serve. You have lots of options for the menu, but you won't end up serving hot dogs with cranberry sauce.

MISSIONS AND GOALS

A lot of stress is laid on goals these days. Being "goal-oriented" is seen as a requisite for business and academic success. Some activities and professions have fallen out of favor because they don't seem to offer a goal, an identifiable, measurable standard of achievement. They just "go on and on."

It's time to reframe our thinking, not only about where we're going but how we're going.

> Where you want to end up is your *goal*.
> What you want to be doing is your *mission*.

Losing ten pounds is a goal, but being healthy is a mission. A dieter with a mission will not give up, while a dieter with a goal can easily fail. Getting a promotion is a goal, but being a valuable, effective worker is a mission. Possessing knowledge or earning a degree is a goal, but learning is a mission. Goals have a way of eluding us, of fulfilling us less than we had hoped when we reach them, but missions never stop giving satisfaction. When you have both goals and missions, you have two sources of strength and pleasure. Then you can't fail.

WHAT IS YOUR MISSION?

Explore the difference between missions and goals by supplying the missing part to the combinations below:

Goal	Mission
Earn a law degree.	_____
Cook dinner.	_____
Marry John (or Susan).	_____
Make $100,000 a year.	_____
Own my own business.	_____

Goal	Mission
————————————	Raise healthy children.
————————————	Provide security for my family.
————————————	Be a good friend, develop joyful relationships.
————————————	Make my community a better place.
————————————	Help others.

(There are no wrong answers.)

GETTING ORGANIZED

The first step to any plan is organization. How aware are you of your organizing ability? Can you handle more than one task at a time? Here are some intriguing exercises devised by the early 20th century mentalist, Harry Kahne, who was able to write five separate words at the same time, using chalk attached to both hands, both feet, and a pointer held between his teeth. He could write these words in any combination of right-side-up, upside-down, and in mirror writing.

Even if you don't want to attempt this feat, you'll still be pleasurably surprised at how facile you can become with everyday tasks by practicing his simultaneous-organizing techniques.

1. Write one three-letter word while spelling another three-letter word out loud at the same time.

write	CAT	JOG	DIP	SAT	POT
spell	DOG	RUN	ARK	END	MAN

2. As you write a three-letter word, spell it out loud in reverse at the same time.

write	FIB	RAT	LOG	PAL	MAD
say	BIF	TAR	GOL	LAP	DAM

3. Write one three-letter word backward while spelling another forward at the same time.

write	TUO	FFO	GID	PIL	RAB
say	FIX	BIT	CAR	SET	FUR

4. Make a list of ten items in each of the following categories:

States	Parts of the Body	Vegetables
1. _____	1. _____	1. _____
2. _____	2. _____	2. _____
3. _____	3. _____	3. _____
4. _____	4. _____	4. _____
5. _____	5. _____	5. _____
6. _____	6. _____	6. _____
7. _____	7. _____	7. _____
8. _____	8. _____	8. _____
9. _____	9. _____	9. _____
10. _____	10. _____	10. _____

Now, cover the list and write all of these words you can remember, spelling them backward.

5. Write down any 20 four-letter words. Study the list. Then write down as many of them as you can remember. Repeat the process, writing as many words as you can remember and spelling them backward.

6. Study a pair of words below. Then shut your eyes and write both words on a piece of paper, but write the top word forward and the bottom word backward, integrating the letters. For instance,

SLAM

PORT becomes   **S**   T   **L**   R   **A**   O   **M**   P

BARK	PUSH	SEND	FAIR	DOVE
FLEE	FLAT	PICK	STOW	LAMB

SEQUENCING

Time management and scheduling is a primary sequencing task of the Organizing Mind. Everyone who gets dressed in the morning, who goes on a trip, cooks a meal, plans a party, or plants a garden must sequence the activities and perform them in a carefully timed sequence.

Here are some sequencing sprints. Look at the list below and then arrange them in order under each heading. Have fun doing it.

Albuquerque   adder
Antarctica   Alpha Centauri
acrobat   apple
amethyst

Biggest to Smallest	Alphabetically	Coldest to Hottest
1. _____	_____	_____
2. _____	_____	_____
3. _____	_____	_____
4. _____	_____	_____
5. _____	_____	_____
6. _____	_____	_____
7. _____	_____	_____

Were any of the sequences easier than the others? Is sequencing something you do without thinking or does it take a real effort? If it's a task that routinely gives you trouble, plot some ways to use your natural ability to notice and your curiosity to boost your organizing ability. When unexpected situations arise, go into a trance or get a good night's sleep, then use Selective Forgetting to let the most important things bubble to the surface.

Answers

	Biggest to Smallest	Alphabetically	Coldest to Hottest
1.	Alpha Centauri	acrobat	Antarctica
2.	Antarctica	adder	amethyst
3.	Albuquerque	Albuquerque	apple
4.	acrobat	Alpha Centauri	adder

Biggest to Smallest	Alphabetically	Coldest to Hottest
5. adder	amethyst	acrobat
6. apple	Antarctica	Albuquerque
7. amethyst	apple	Alpha Centauri

An efficient organizer can weigh different factors and decide on a sensible course of action. Some people are more easily distracted than others by conversations among the parts of their mind. The great showman, Florenz Ziegfeld, would offer such high salaries to the stars of the *Ziegfeld Follies* and spend so much on the production that, even if every seat were filled for every performance, he would lose money each week the show ran. The more successful the show, the more money he lost. His emotions said "I want to do the most magnificent stage production ever," and his practical mind ignored the financial implausibility. Here are some other improbable situations. See how well you can organize the information to come up with a solution.

1. This is an oldie. You want to cross a river with a fox, a goose, and a bag of grain. There is a small boat, operated by pulling a rope from either shore, which will hold only two items at a time. You cannot leave the fox alone with the goose or he will eat it. You cannot leave the goose alone with the grain or she will eat it. How do you get yourself and your unlikely possessions across? What is the most efficient way you can organize your trip?

2. You are making a tour of places starting with the letter *C*. What is your shortest route? You may start in any city and finish in any other city.

Chicago	Cairo
Calcutta	Cheyenne
Calgary	Canton
Calais	Caracas

3. You are sitting quietly on a large, comfortable sofa, cutting out paper dolls, when suddenly your dog runs into the room, carrying a stick of dynamite in its mouth.

The fuse is lit and has only two inches to go before reaching the dynamite. In the room with you is your lifetime collection of rare porcelains. Below your open window, a group of children are playing in a wading pool. Ten feet away, down the hall, is a laundry chute to the basement. Thirty feet away, at the back of the house, is a window overlooking an abandoned mine shaft. What do you do?

Answers

1. Four round trips. (1) Take goose across and return alone. (2) Take grain across, leave it, and return with goose. (3) Leave goose, take fox across, leave fox with the grain, and return alone. (4) Take the goose across and all of you go on your way. (Impatient souls may enjoy more variations on this puzzle in chapter 7.)

2. Caracas, Chicago, Cheyenne, Calgary, Calais, Cairo, Calcutta, Canton (or reverse order)

3. Cut off the fuse with your scissors.

GETTING STARTED: ENERGIZING YOURSELF

When people grumble about their lack of energy, the complaint usually stems from one of the following:

- Procrastinating

- Feeling overwhelmed

- Reduced efficiency from stress

- Reduced efficiency from depression

- Actual fatigue (caused by hard work or illness)

PROCRASTINATION

Jeff says: "There's always time tomorrow. Everybody nags at me about doing things, but I just can't seem to get to them all. I promise myself that I'll do twice as much next time to make up for not doing it this time, and then it gets so out of hand that I end up not doing anything at all."

Procrastination can be the result of mental conflict or it can be just a bad habit. If you are almost certain to get out of doing something you don't want to do by putting it off, that's not procrastination. That's just smart. Napoleon was said to answer his mail only once a month because he found that many of the problems solved themselves during the delay.

To qualify as procrastination, your failure to act must possess two qualities:

1. It must be irrational.

2. It must be harmful to you or others in some way.

For some people, procrastination may represent direct or indirect rebellion against authority. Others simply enjoy the fantasy of potential. Like Lady Catherine de Bourgh in Jane Austen's *Pride and Prejudice*, we are certain we could play the piano exquisitely, had we ever bothered to learn. This can be a relatively harmless self-deception or a major block to growth.

So many of us sigh and say, "If only I could do that, but I doubt that I'd be very good at it . . . " So we sit and do nothing. If we can't sail around the world, we don't plan a trip to the next state. If we can't play at Carnegie Hall, we don't take piano lessons. If we can't change the world, we lock the door and turn on the television. Remember, if a thing is worth doing, it is worth doing *badly.*

Some people employ a kind of unconscious magical thinking: "If I don't finish this project, there will always be more time to do it later. (Therefore, I won't die.)" A common example is putting off making a will, even though most would agree that one of their life's missions is to care for those they love. A more eccentric and much less harmful example of this concept is the labyrinthine Winchester Mystery House in San Jose, California. Its owner supposedly believed that she wouldn't die as long as she kept adding rooms to her house. (Of course, she may just have enjoyed the stimulation of designing and of supervising craftsmen.) But many of us put off traveling, writing, building, even organizing our own possessions and affairs because we want to believe that there will always be time to do it later.

For some people, putting things off acts as a valuable protection against being judged by the result of their efforts. Their critical inner voice is muttering, "That's not good enough . . . ," or they fear the criticism of others. They are convinced that performance equals ability and ability equals self-worth. "If I never finish," they reason, "I will never fail." These people should not give up the self-protection of procrastination until they are sure they are able to protect their most valuable asset, their self-esteem.

Fill in the blank: "I'm no good at _____."

Your mind's executive side is making this statement. You may believe this evaluation is very reasonable, based on what you think you have observed about yourself and on the popular misconception that your talents are fixed at birth so it's no use struggling to change them. But that's not your excuse, that's your *problem*. You can not only learn to be smarter, you can learn to *work* smarter.

For most chronic procrastinators, simple time management techniques will do little to overcome the problem. These people need to attack the source of their insecurity or conflict. However, insight alone is not sufficient to motivate change. Discovering *why* you are blocking yourself is a valuable first step, but in itself it won't end procrastination.

Try appealing to your sense of wonder to overcome the discomfort being provided by your emotions. Psychologist Richard Bandler, in his book *Using Your Brain—For a Change,* describes a technique to melt preconceptions. He calls it *integrating anchors.* Here's how it works:

First, look at what you wrote above. Select something that represents your problem. Position yourself where you can see this thing that you're not good at—a page of puzzling math, a complicated writing project, a photo of a person particularly difficult for you to deal with, the messy garage you can't seem to organize, a map you find inscrutable, a complicated appliance you can't operate properly. We'll call this object your "nemesis."

Now close your eyes and think of a time when you were very excited and dying of curiosity, a tremendously pleasurable experience. Take your time to choose something that really gave you delight. Savor that moment. Feel yourself starting to glow.

Now open your eyes and look at your nemesis for just a second or two. Quickly close your eyes and think of the pleasurable experience again. Repeat this process until the two experiences begin to overlap and become integrated, so that the pleasurable glow remains when you look at your nemesis.

Then test yourself. Stare into space and think of a neutral experience. Then look at your nemesis. How do you feel about it now? Do you get a sudden rush of pleasurable anticipation? This is a simple example of Richard Bandler's neuro-linguistic programming techniques. Some are much more elaborate and very effective for erasing major phobias and neuroses.

OVERBOOKED AND OVERWHELMED

Bev says: "There's never enough time! I'm always late. Late to work, to class, to bed. Late with car payments, with paper work on my job, with birthday cards, with everything. Sometimes I think if one more thing happens to mess up my schedule, I'll die. Then my furnace blows up, I'm told I have to take another night course to maintain my accreditation, and my supervisor gets sick so I have to take on his job, too."

Bev may be the victim of circumstances. Then again, she may be a compulsive overbooker who can't bear to experience an empty moment. There are several varieties of people who routinely overbook themselves.

The Optimist. Basically realistic, he schedules himself with no time for anything to go wrong. Some days his optimism is rewarded. Some days it isn't.

The Self-Discipliner. "I am so innately lazy that I'll never accomplish *anything* if I don't build up enormous outside pressure," this person reasons. So she fills her calendar to the brim. (She also enjoys a secret sense of self-importance that she is in so much demand.)

The Ostrich. This person blocks a painful personal problem or relationship by being too busy to stop and think about it. A lull in activity sends him or her frantically searching for something to do. This intense level of activity is a way commonly used to cope with grief effectively until the pain subsides to manageable proportions, but for most other problems it only postpones dealing with the inevitable.

The Yes-er. Some overbooked people are so reluctant to refuse any request that they agree to things they probably can't accomplish. These people who Can't-Say-No actually fall into several categories.

- The cowardly yes-er—So eager to avoid the immediate unpleasantness of a refusal that he says yes to anything (and then faces much more unpleasantness later).

- The thrill-seeking yes-er—She experiences exhilaration from the gratitude of the requester and from the fleeting, if false, sense of power she gets as she imagines herself actually carrying out the request.

- The status yes-er—He says yes to any request that supports his self-image—the powerful administrator, the brilliant scholar, the socially prominent party giver, the philanthropist.

- The good-old-so-and-so yes-er—To feel like a good, strong, and worthwhile person, this yes-er must say yes to any request for assistance. (The difference between the status yes-er and good-old-so-and-so is that the status yes-er must receive public recognition and esteem in exchange for her "yes" while good-old-so-and-so is content with feelings of self-worth.)

- The poor-little-me yes-er—A negative version of both the status and good-old-so-and-so yes-ers, this person agrees to anything that promotes a negative self-image: family slave, office flunky, school stooge. The difference is that, for poor-little-me, the payoff is *bad* feelings and *loss* of esteem, confirming a self-image as a doormat.

The Magical Thinker. An eccentric relative of the overly opti-
mistic optimist, the magical thinker genuinely hopes that this time
he'll be able to carry it off. Generally, he is convinced that some
powerful outside force makes traffic lights turn green, elevator doors
open, and empty cabs pull up whenever he wishes. When they don't,
it is taken as proof of the iniquity of his enemies, or a sign that one of
his personal faults has been recognized and punished by the gods.

The Truly-Trapped Person. Occasionally people are actually
victims of circumstances. They may need to work long hours to
survive and care for their loved ones, or to juggle conflicting and
unavoidable responsibilities. Ironically, these are the people who
most often reframe their perceptions, temporarily or even permanently,
so that what they get is what they want. They are rarely among the
complainers because they find satisfaction and personal growth in
their efforts.

Sometimes life dumps too much on us. This happens to everyone *sometimes*, but when it happens *all* the time, over and over to the
same someone, and that someone constantly complains about it and
feels overwhelmed, it's time to examine the cause.

Try a reality check: Do you frequently overestimate your time
and energy? Can you consciously cut back? If not, why not?
Unrealistic demands from others? From yourself? Can you negotiate
with others? With yourself? Let's look at Bev in the example above.

Bev was the eldest of five children. Her parents worked long
hours in their small store, and Bev got lots of praise from them for
taking care of the younger children, helping out in the store, and
keeping up with her school work as well. She felt much appreciated
for what she did. Ironically her parents were setting up a pattern
that could cause problems in her adult life, because she did *not* feel
appreciated for what she *was*. No one ever said: "How wonderful
that you are you! Sit down and tell me what you think and feel." She
equated her self-worth with what she could produce, not what she
thought or felt or loved or admired.

Often the eldest child, like Bev, will become "parentized" and
go through life being a pseudo-parent to others, supportive, nurturing,
a tower of strength, but rarely offering her own thoughts and
problems for discussion.

When I met Bev, she said she was exhausted and she certainly
looked it. She had risen at 4:00 A.M. that morning, done the house-

work, taken her children to school, then worked eight hours at a very demanding job as a specialized physical therapist, lifting, moving, and exercising people who were frequently in pain and sometimes dangerously irrational. After work she shopped for groceries, picked up her children, cooked and served dinner, and supervised homework. In her spare time she did major home repairs, ran her recalcitrant car to and from the repair shop, attended an average of one evening meeting a week (PTA, job-related, clubs, etc.). She worked every other Saturday as well, and on Sundays she sometimes cared for a number of children to fulfill her obligation to her neighborhood baby-sitting pool.

Rather than being the stereotypical Super Mom, Bev had run herself down to where she said she got little pleasure from her home, children, job, or club activities. I had to fight a smile when she admitted that she had been the eldest in a large family. I had to stifle a cry of amazement when she proudly announced that everything would be all right now—she had just joined a health club and signed up for two weekly exercise classes so she could "meet interesting people." Why are other people's problems always so obvious to others, but rarely to those involved? That's where the skill of the therapist comes in.

I asked Bev how much socializing the exercise class people did. Did they all go out for coffee together after the class, for example? "No," she said. "Even if they did, I couldn't go with them. I have to get right home."

Then I asked about her job and her family. She glowed as she described them. She was proud of her children and seemed like a genuinely compassionate and talented person, well regarded by her coworkers and patients. She loved working on her fixer-upper house and rejected a suggestion that she replace her cranky old car: "Lulubelle is like one of the family." She did not seem to need to "reframe" her view of her life because it was fairly positive. I suspected briefly that she might be playing the game called "You-can't-help-me-no-matter-how-hard-you-try!" but that wasn't so. She seemed genuinely puzzled by her predicament.

I zeroed in on her comment about "meeting interesting people." What kind of socializing did she do? The list was lengthy but all business-related or club-related. There were affairs she "had" to attend, and sometimes high-energy reunions with people she had known in previous jobs or in college—nothing that would promote intimacy or provide support for her as a person. She had a large circle of friends, most of whom came to her for comfort and advice. I began to suspect that her search for "interesting people" meant people who would be interested in *her,* but she was either inept or ambivalent in her efforts to find them.

"How would you feel about spending some time with one of your friends and just talking?"

"Oh, I do that already."

"What about?"

"Their problems. Their projects. Sometimes a project that we are doing together."

"What about *your* problems?"

"I don't know what you mean."

"Your problems—like trying to do too much all the time."

"Oh, that's not a problem. . . ." She paused, suddenly aware of the contradiction. She was worn out but the powerful internal executive element of her mind didn't want to admit that anything was wrong. Just telling her my ideas wouldn't have worked. I decided to show her another way to feel about herself.

"I have a new exercise for you," I said. "Once a week, I want you to pick up the phone and call one of your friends. When she says, "How are you?" tell her how you are feeling. Explain that you are not looking for solutions or praise, just someone to listen. See if she can do that. If she starts to ask your advice, gently steer her back to you. If you can't keep the conversation on you and your feelings, try a different friend."

Bev was naturally very skeptical: "I don't see the point." I wasn't sure she'd try it.

Several weeks later she reported that she had actually had several such conversations. "How did you feel?" I asked.

"Silly! And . . . "

"And?"

"Kind of good. Relaxed a little."

"So it feels good when someone else just listens to you?" (Long before psychology was invented, barbers, bartenders, and hairdressers recognized the powerful therapeutic powers of being a good listener.) Bev indicated she would probably continue initiating these more intimate conversations in which she could get as well as give nurturing.

Then I explained my strategy: that she was identifying people who were impressed by and cared about *her* as well as what she accomplishes. She knew many of these people already but hadn't recognized them or learned to ask them for what she needed. I suggested that when she could get recognition for just being herself, she wouldn't need to be busy all the time to feel good about herself.

DEPRESSION

> Michael says: "I'm tired all the time; drag myself to
> work, fall into bed at 8 o'clock, can't make decisions.
> I've tried vitamins and been to the doctor. He says I
> need a psychiatrist, but I think *that's* crazy. There
> must be something physically wrong with me. I just
> have no energy."

There *may* be something physically wrong with Michael, but after most physical reasons have been overruled, it's time to consider temporary or chronic depression. Mild depression can be nature's way of offering a renewal time, a slowing down before new growth, the *yin* to contrast with the coming *yang*. Some depressions are so complex and deeply entrenched that they require professional therapy to overcome. However, if you suspect that you are suffering from the everyday "Blue Monday blahs," try offering each part of your mind some rest and recreation. (Depression is discussed more extensively in chapter 11.)

First, respond to your feelings. Savor your dark mood. Really enjoy it because it's so fleeting and temporary. Then choose one of the exercises on page 58, whichever one suits your fancy.

• **Hibernate.** At a time when you should be busiest, retreat to a private space. Hire a baby-sitter. Call in sick. (You are!) Now draw the curtains, unplug the phone, snuggle under the covers. Sleep. Read. Eat. (No TV, please, it's too hypnotic.) Feel incredibly pampered. And isolated. Do this for at least four hours. Are you getting bored? Want to continue? If you're still going, stop after eight hours. If you feel like you'd like to continue, schedule a renewal time every week or so.

• **Go fishing.** Figuratively is fine. The process of going fishing represents renewal. As the first step, you change your clothes to something comfortable and a bit eccentric, something you only wear when you are going to do something to please yourself.

   Then you concentrate intensely on some small objects that you'll be taking with you. They could be fishing lures. They could be treats for a gourmet solo picnic, subway or road maps for a trip to an unfamiliar place, a bird book or rock guide for a walk through a park or the countryside. Intense concentration is essential as step two, a kind of contraction before release.

   Step three is the activity itself. Here's where the fun comes in. You are "doing something" but you're really doing nothing. Your mind can flit back and forth between the illusory fish and your own thoughts. The unique thing about "fishing" is that it has a definite purpose (catching a fish) but it still succeeds as an activity even if no fish appear. The process is independent of the product. You have bought valuable time to let your mind drift, exploring fancies, perhaps darting toward a painful or difficult problem, then skipping away, only to return later for a more searching examination. Nothing is forced. Always there is the safety of concentrating on the fish. And no one can criticize you for being unproductive. After all, you are *fishing*.

• **Play a game.** Preferably with a child, but even solitaire is okay. Focus totally on the game. Not on winning, but on playing. Make up silly rules: you can only throw the basketball while standing on your left foot; play chess and whinny whenever you move a knight, sing a hymn when moving a bishop; in poker, all spades are wild cards; four strikes equal a walk. Stop playing when you are laughing too hard to continue.

REAL FATIGUE

It used to be popular to suffer nervous breakdowns from overwork. Now both terms are somewhat obsolete. We know that hard work is invigorating and that the fatigue that follows strenuous physical or mental exercise is quite pleasurable. The negative, debilitating kind of fatigue comes from frustration and stress—tension with nowhere to go.

So unless you have a physical disability that makes exercise dangerous, or your body is worn down by poor nutrition, lack of adequate exercise and rest, or substance abuse, fatigue should be a welcome and healthful part of the energy-work-rest cycle.

Some of the people who complain of chronic fatigue are the same ones who take sleeping pills to turn off their busy minds and twitching muscles at bedtime. Others wake up "still as tired as when I went to bed" because they have slept poorly. What these people need is not less activity but more. A run, a swim, or a brisk walk in the evening, or even some in-place aerobics in a wheelchair. Then an involving book, a crossword puzzle, a complex knitting pattern, or drafting project for a new gadget. Nothing that involves any sense of personal worth, just intense involvement with something fun and rather abstract. Finally, as the muscles relax and go slack, the mind turns over some pleasantly engrossing bits of color and pattern, protecting it from assault by the cares of the day. Then sleep.

CURIOSITY AS A SOURCE OF ENERGY

Your most potent energizer is the wondering part of your mind. It has literally kept people alive—"I won't die until after the World

Series!"—in hospital beds, in dank prison cells, marooned on desert islands. There is nothing more potent than the adrenaline rush of curiosity. When your energy flags, give your curiosity a poke. Enliven boring routines with mental high jinks: "Is he wearing a toupee?" "What's in her shopping cart?" "Can I hold my breath until he gets to the point of his speech?" Find the fun in difficult tasks. If there is none, make it up:

"I'm too tired to wash my hair tonight."
(*I wonder what that new shampoo smells like!*)

"I'll wash the dishes in the morning."
(*I wonder if I could figure out a technique for doing simple aerobics while washing dishes. A video of that would make me a fortune!*)

"Next week I'll visit Aunt Millie *twice* to make up for missing this week." (Aunt Millie is sometimes difficult.)
(*I wonder if she remembers that picnic we went on together when I was a kid—the bull that chased us and the salamanders I caught. She lent me a mayonnaise jar to bring them home. . . .*)

Choose only enjoyable tasks. Not possible? Then figure out ways to enjoy tasks you must do. You're no dummy! If you're clever enough to know what needs to be done, you're clever enough to frame all the steps so that you can derive some pleasure and satisfaction from them. If absolutely necessary, concentrate on the goal rather than how you are reaching it; but making the journey itself pleasurable and rewarding is much safer. Suppose you never reach the goal, or decide, when you do reach it, that you don't want it after all. If the process is enriching, the final result matters less.

Between 1840 and 1870, up to a half million people made the journey across America to settle the West. Many underwent terrible hardships. Many died. The letters and diaries of those who reached California sometimes indicated the trip had not been worth it. One settler, Mary Powers, wrote in her journal, "If anyone should ask my advice about coming to this country in that way, I should say, 'Take a good dose of arsenic one week before you think of starting. Your death would be speedier and easier and your friends would have more comfort in knowing where your bones were reposing.'"

All that suffering to get to a place they didn't even like! Not every journey can be gratifying—studying or starting a business or even returning to health after a devastating illness can be arduous and exhausting—but you still have choices about what you hope for and what you remember. People who look up at the night sky can see mostly darkness, or they can see the stars.

MAXIMUM POTENTIAL

Your mind came into existence able to do a multitude of things. When there is no need for a particular ability, that ability withers away, just like an unused muscle. Nearly every child is born with the ability to speak every sound in every language known to mankind, but most of the sounds aren't needed and are quickly discarded and forgotten.

We used to hear a lot about how we used only a small portion of our brains. This was because large areas were still terra incognita, unmapped by scientists. Now they are mapped and we know that all the brain works all the time in some way or other.

Nearly everyone wants to work to full potential. As the natural resources of the earth get used up, the mind seems to be one of the last frontiers for exploration and exploitation. A number of self-improvement programs have emerged to encourage a personal vision of achievement, even a sort of grandiosity.

Steve DeVore, founder of SyberVision Systems, Inc., a source for how-to videotapes, describes "high achievers":

> High achievers have a sense of almost believing in
> themselves as possessing godlike abilities, that noth-
> ing is impossible. They believe that almost to the
> point of having control over their environment. . . .
> Saying, "Nothing is impossible for me—I possess the
> intelligence of a god."

Since no one has yet figured out how to evaluate or assess the intelligence of a god, most of us are delighted to possess the intelligence of a human. "The mind of man is capable of anything," said Joseph Conrad in *Heart of Darkness,* "because everything is in it, all the past as well as all the future."

Hopefully that intelligence allows us to notice when well-intentioned systems for mind development segue into mind control. The mind-control cults of today may have new gimmicks, new technology, but they are not new. Since prehistory there has usually been someone around to say, "You are not thinking efficiently. I'll show you how to think. In fact, let me think for you."

In his best seller, *Iacocca*, Lee Iacocca says, "There's a world of difference between a strong ego, which is essential, and a large ego which can be destructive. . . ." We humans walk a precarious line between self-confidence and grandiosity, between curiosity and gullibility.

ENERGIZING YOUR MIND

As you have discovered, each part of your mind has a different agenda. If they are to work together like a team of champion rowers, you need to offer each of your different facets a slightly different motivation, plus cyclical periods of activity and rest.

 **meeting of the minds**

Executive Part: A sense of control, prestige, accomplishment, an unthreatening goal. (Sometimes the other parts of the mind conspire to make the Executive Mind feel good even in a bad situation; this is called "self-confidence.")

Wondering Part: Exploration, play, fun. ("Wow!")

Organizing Part: Things to sort and judge and analyze and fuss over. ("Hmmmm.") Tasks that do not violate your *Manual of Procedures.* (When this happens, something usually feels "wrong" or you experience a "gut reaction." Turning off the critical part of your mind can get you through the task, but you may get emotional feedback in the form of guilt.) A schedule or routine that your organizing ability genuinely accepts as workable and accomplishable. (Overload incites rebellion.)

Reacting Part: Emotional security and fulfillment. (If action may threaten emotional safety and sense of self, this must be dealt with!) Opportunity for an appropriate range of emotional responses that support the main purpose. (Anger and sorrow can be positive motivators just as much as joy and contentment.)

Knowing Part: A wide range of intellectual opportunities and stimulation. (This is why many people take classes, go back to school, or change professions.) Enhancing visual, aural, and tactile stimulation, supported by a healthy, in-tune body, to provide a sense of general well-being.

No one task, no one day has to satisfy every mind totally, but when you find your psychic energy constantly lagging, it's a good bet that the needs of one or more of the minds aren't being met. It's no coincidence that philosophers from Plato to Benjamin Franklin have lauded the well-rounded man. Even the U.S. armed forces have formalized the practice of "R & R" (Rest and Recreation) to revitalize fighting troops.

For maximum mental energy, look for unmet needs and decide how to fill them. To get the most out of your mind, check that it is getting the most out of you.

PROCRASTINATION

When do you have trouble getting started? What is your most frequent procrastination problem? _____

_____

_____

Check your favorite excuse:
- ☐ I'll wait until I'm inspired to start.
- ☐ I've been working so hard, I think I'll take a break first.
- ☐ I don't have everything I need to begin.
- ☐ I don't have enough time to finish right now. I'll wait till I can do it all at once.
- ☐ I'm too tired. I'll start again in the morning.
- ☐ Other _____

Your first step should be to apply simple time management techniques to the problem. There are dozens of good books on time management, listing logical steps for organizing your resources. (However, if this were your strength, would you be reading this chapter?)

Are you putting off a job because it seems to require too large a block of time? If so, use the Swiss Cheese technique Alan Lakein describes in *How to Get Control of Your Time and Your Life.* Poke holes in the job, dividing it up into small bits that can be accomplished in a few minutes. Write a schedule for completing each small piece and stick to it. If that seems too complicated, try Dr. Neil Fiore's "Un-Schedule" schedule. In his book, *The Now Habit,* he advises: commit any time not specifically scheduled for other activities to the project, and reward yourself for each fifteen minutes you put in.

THE TEN-MINUTE TECHNIQUE

In my "Free Yourself to Write" seminars, I use a Ten-Minute Technique that has converted hundreds of procrastinators. "Oh, I could never write a book," they say. Then I sit them down and tell them to write for only ten minutes. "Write anything at all. Your shopping list, the names of your golf buddies. Do not lift the pen from the paper. (Or, for later at home: Do not stop typing even for a few seconds.) If you get stuck, just write the last word over and over until something new comes to you."

Then I set a timer. You can bet that at the end of the ten minutes very few want to put down their pens. All have produced two pages or more, and much of what they have produced surprises and delights them.

Two pages a day is 14 pages a week, 60 pages a month, 720 pages a year . . . assuming you can stop at just two pages. All for an amount of time that most of us spend waiting for the kettle to boil.

Even if you don't want to write, this same technique works for housework, income tax, gardening. There are few tasks that can't be tamed by the Ten-Minute Technique!

THE FIVE-MIND APPROACH

If time management isn't an issue, discussing the problem with the five parts of the mind can be helpful. (To refresh yourself on their specific roles see page 6.) Here is a sample "conversation."

 **meeting of the minds**

Executive Part: "I really should make a will."

Organizing Part: "If I die without a will, it will take a lot of time and trouble for other people to straighten out my affairs. My personal possessions might go to the city dump and my money to the state."

So far we have agreement. But let's keep listening.

Reacting Part: "I'm not going to die! And lawyers are so intimidating. I don't need a will. I have years before I need to think about such things."

Wondering Part: "Yeah, making wills means you're going to die. There are too many urgent things to think about."

Knowing Part: "I've heard horror stories about the losses and difficulties when people don't have wills. I agree that a will is a good precaution. But I don't know where to start."

Wondering Part: "I can't afford a fancy lawyer." (*runs some mental movies of Perry Mason's posh office*) "What if I'm cheated?" (*recalls a newspaper article about a crooked lawyer*) "Or I look like a fool?" (*relives childhood script of disapproving authority figure*) "Maybe I could just write down some things and leave the note in my desk. . . . I should get a book at the library to see how to do that."

It becomes obvious that the wondering and reacting parts of the mind are very good at protecting us by blocking unpleasant activities. Since writing a will or, to a lesser extent, buying insurance reminds us that we may not be immortal, this is a common discomfort area. Once we recognize that our guardians are being overprotective, we can enlist their help in the project:

Executive Part: "Think how good we'll feel when all those pesky details are worked out. A neat blue folder of typed pages showing my friends and family how I care about them. What freedom, what peace of mind! Imagine them stricken with grief and then finding that I've planned everything so carefully that they can easily carry out my wishes."

(If the wondering and reacting parts balk at this, you might suspect some hostility toward the potential survivors. Then switch tactics and think of giving those folks a spectral Bronx cheer from the beyond: "You thought I'd make a mess of things and I fooled you!" Learn to recognize your prejudices instead of denying them, and then to work with the reality.)

Wondering Part: "I'll convince myself that *having* a will means that nothing can happen to me. I'll get excited about finding out the best way to go about this. Talk to other people. Read some books. Call the Bar Association for a recommendation."

Organizing Part: (*recognizing a familiar pattern*) "Better give yourself a deadline or you'll research into the next century and never do anything."

Executive Part: "Time for some bribery. As soon as my will is done, I'll start planning my vacation." (*or some other pleasurable activity*)

Reacting Part: "When I think about a will, I'll feel that it's a part of my immortality—a document about me that will exist for centuries to come. I want it to be good!"

Wondering Part: "I'll get some books on wills and some travel books at the library, but I won't open the travel books until I've got my will signed and sealed. Maybe a boat down the Mississippi this year, or the Canadian Rockies . . . or what about China!"

And the wondering part pulls you past the point of resistance by giving you a glowing goal beyond.

Does procrastination get in your way? Maybe you are ready to give up the protection and do things a different way. Try discussing the situation with the five parts of your mind, using the example above as a guide. What do each of them really think of the specific task you are procrastinating about? *Listen carefully.*

What the Parts of Your Mind Say:

Executive Part: I should/must do this because _____

_____

Wondering Part: _____

_____

Organizing Part: _____

_____

Reacting Part: _____

_____

Knowing Part: _____

_____

Any clues? Do you know any facts that indicate some of your attitudes may be outdated? Can you suspend premature critical judgment that may be preventing you from starting? Can you come up with fresh solutions? Can you choose to interpret the situation differently or provide new observations? Can you choose a different emotional response—joy instead of fear, patience instead of anger? Can your Executive Mind alter its original directive?

Try offering yourself rewards for cooperating. Things your mind really wants and needs, not something you "should" want. Stop harassing yourself. Forget all the critical messages you have been giving yourself. Tell that part of your mind, "Thank you very much for pointing that problem out to me, and now I need your energy for change."

What deals would you like to make with yourself? Jot them down as offers you can't refuse:

For your curiosity and sense of wonder: _____

For your analytic ability: _____

For your emotions: _____

For your senses: _____

For your overseeing executive: _____

Will you try these deals? If not, back up and change them to something more realistic, more appealing, more innovative.

TAKING CONTROL

You can make powerful steps toward taking control of your schedule by answering one simple question: *What is the purpose of your life?*

When you have an answer to that question, you have the key to controlling your time and activities. All the lists and charts and datebooks can't do as much to organize you as you can yourself by knowing who you are and what you want to do.

CONCENTRATING: HOW TO FOCUS YOURSELF

Pat says: "I just can't seem to concentrate. My mind works like a hamster wheel, spinning around and never going anywhere. I get some great ideas, but then I never finish deciding what to do."

Paul says: "How can I think more efficiently? I wool-gather and don't focus on the problem I want to solve. Or I try to do too many things at once and end up not doing any of them well."

Using the human mind in a focused, concentrated way is a relatively recent development. Early man had to remain open to every outside stimulus, alert for changes around him that might mean peril. He had little need or motive to notice only one thing to the exclusion of others.

Today, selective attention has become essential for performing many tasks. This concentration on one thing while ignoring all diversions requires the consent of each part of the mind. Since each part has a different agenda, you need to get all of them to agree that focusing on this one thing is in their own best interest. You are like a skillful teacher, who needs to find some element about this thing to interest each student.

Focusing on just one thing is like listening to a conversation at a noisy party or one voice among the static and cross-signals of a CB radio. It's relatively easy to listen to that one voice if none of the interference is interesting, much harder if a more fascinating conversation is also going on.

Most people can concentrate on what affects them most. Dr. Samuel Johnson noted in 1777 that, "When a man knows he is to be hanged in a fortnight, it concentrates his mind wonderfully." Imagine that you are in a plummeting elevator and someone is shouting instructions to you over the emergency telephone. Would you be likely to allow any distraction to keep you from learning those instructions? Probably not.

The concentration that most of us would like to have is the conscious, focused attention that blocks outside distractions and permits maximum responsiveness, even when the project at hand is not the most important or interesting thing in life. People who can reach this level of intense energy do so through strategies that may seem frivolous to the less disciplined. Plainly put, they make a game out of work.

Our selective attention when we play is phenomenal. The fun and excitement of the moment can easily block most outside stimuli, even physical pain. Resourceful people devise ways to make boring but necessary tasks a playful challenge until the tasks have become ingrained habits.

Using a let's-have-fun, game-oriented framework can produce a remarkable state of total concentration. In one experiment done at Cornell University, volunteers were shown a videotape of a basketball game and told to press a key whenever the ball changed hands. Afterwards, according to the report in *Cognitive Psychology,* they were asked if they had noticed anything unusual. Very few of the viewers could recall anything out of the ordinary. They were astounded when the tape was replayed and they noticed for the first time that a young woman in a skirt had changed places with one of the male basketball players. The intensity of the viewers' task had blocked any information that did not fit in.

Here are some common situations and playful strategies for enhancing concentration.

"The phone keeps ringing, the kids are yelling, and I've got to balance my checkbook before I go shopping."

(*"Hey, kids, what's $43.87 take away $15.66? Get some paper and help me. Let's see if we can do the problem before the phone rings again!" Even if the kids don't pitch in, this is sure to quiet them.*)

"I've got to finish reading this report, but I'm hungry and I keep thinking about a disturbing conversation I had with a friend yesterday."

(*If possible, take a big drink of water or have a small snack. Stretch, breathe deeply. Then imagine your friend very vividly. Her mouth is moving. Listen! She is reading the report out loud! As your eye passes over the words, you hear her voice. If she switches to your disturbing conversation, imagine the report stuffed in her mouth until she is back on track. If she is really bothering you, imagine that someone more exciting, more supportive of you is reading the report to you, drowning her out.*)

"One minute I'm thinking about a problem at work. Then I'm thinking about whether I should take the car in to the garage, then about my aunt who hasn't been in great health lately. My mind seems to jump from one thing to another and I never finish a thought."

(*Drifting thoughts often come up with some terrific insights, but if you want to focus long enough to actually think something through, try this game. Give yourself permission to think of four consecutive things. Then make a list of them—mentally or on paper. Set a time to think about any one of them, the first one that pops out at you as you consider the list. Make the times quite short at first—it takes practice to concentrate for long periods. For instance, I will think about Aunt Clara until the next red light, or, I will think about those sales figures until the kettle boils.*)

Obviously, unless we have a physical problem (such as illness or fatigue) or a severe mental problem, the ability to concentrate is within all of us. The trick is to apply this kind of intensity when, where, and on what we want to.

If you are consistently unable to concentrate on things that should be important to you, if you consistently try to do too many things at once or are sidetracked by unimportant details, you should consider the possibility that some part of your mind has a hidden agenda, a reason to "protect" you with this behavior. These hidden agendas can include blocks caused by unresolved problems in relationships with family or friends, by fear of success or failure, by the desire to punish someone or gain approval or attention, or by the need to "prove" something.

If you think concentration is something unpleasant and arduous, you may never have experienced it. Concentration is pure pleasure. When you are focusing intensely, when you are totally absorbed in what you are doing, you can reach a level of euphoria similar to a "runner's high" or the ecstasy produced by sex or drugs. Time is distorted. Everything is effortless. You have a heightened sense of well-being, even if what you are concentrating on is difficult, dangerous, or unpleasant. You have an intense sense of aliveness, an ability to respond instantly to the shifting demands of the situation.

People who are routinely "transported" by an experience like music or poetry or a hockey game know this feeling well. Even an engrossing book or television program can have this effect. The newspapers reported recently that the members of a family watching the last minutes of a critical episode of *Dallas* had to be forced from their home when it caught fire. (No wonder television commercials are so successful!)

University of Chicago researchers who have been studying concentration for over a decade call this altered consciousness the "flow state." Mihalyi Csikszentmihalyi, Ph.D., professor of behavioral sciences at the university, says that "People seem to concentrate best when the demands on them are a bit greater than usual, and they are able to give more than usual. If there is too little demand on them, people are bored. If there is too much for them to handle, they get anxious."

To achieve this balance, the wondering part of your mind needs to turn off boredom and the executive part needs to turn off anxiety. One assembly line worker in the Chicago study tightened the same screws day after day for years. But he maintained his concentration (and sanity) by constantly trying new ways to do it better and faster. An assembly line worker might become bored with a task, but an efficiency expert, hired to find a better way to do the job, wouldn't. A baby-sitter might get bored with the sameness of her job, but a child psychologist observing children's behavior never would. Boredom lies not in the task but in the *framing* of the task.

Anxiety is harder to overcome than boredom. Healthy fear may accompany a task like trying to crawl along a vine over a pit of crocodiles. Coping with anxiety is discussed further in chapter 11, but basically it involves an agreement between your mental executive and your emotions, using information on the potential danger of the situation and ways to overcome any problems. Sometimes the anxiety comes from the magnitude of the job. It is so huge, so overwhelming, that you find yourself just sitting and wringing your hands. To get back to the "flow," break the task into bite-sized chunks, then experience the high of sailing through each stage on schedule.

Making yourself pay attention doesn't produce euphoria. We record very different brain activity patterns for effortless concentration and forced attention. Forced attention requires greater brain activity, like a car going uphill in first gear. Concentration takes less effort than everyday tasks, like a car cruising downhill. No wonder we are exhausted after a "hard" day, but exhilarated after a "good" one.

The first step toward total concentration is to activate your curiosity and imagination. Pick up a magazine and find a photo or illustration that shows several people. Stare at it and make up a story about what the people are really thinking and doing. Or turn on the TV and find a dramatic or comedy program. Turn off the sound and make up dialogue for the characters.

How long can you stay interested in this activity? The longer you can, the more resourceful you are. If it's hard, give yourself a period of Curiosity Calisthenics every day. When a question pops into your mind, jump on it as though it were a twenty-dollar bill blowing down the street. Look things up. Check them out. ("What *does* that fat man have in his grocery cart?" "*Who* is that pretty, silver-haired lady waiting to meet?")

When you were in school, someone sometime probably told you to "Stop playing and concentrate!" I'm saying *start* playing and concentrate.

The second step in achieving total concentration is noticing things. How aware are you of your surroundings? Rate your skills.

	Always 5	Usually 4	Sometimes 3	Rarely 2	Never 1
Colors affect my mood.	5	4	3	2	1
I can tell the difference between a violin and a cello.	5	4	3	2	1
Ripe fruit looks and smells different from unripe fruit.	5	4	3	2	1
I can tell the difference between brands of _____ (fill in your favorite manu- factured food, i.e., potato chips, wine, hot dogs, chocolate bars) by the taste.	5	4	3	2	1
I recognize music by my favorite com-					

	Always 5	Usually 4	Sometimes 3	Rarely 2	Never 1
posers, even if I've never heard the particular piece before.	5	4	3	2	1
How clothes feel is very important to me.	5	4	3	2	1
I recognize at least a dozen brands of perfume and cologne by their smell.	5	4	3	2	1
New situations often remind me of experiences I have already had.	5	4	3	2	1

How aware of *you* are you? You look at yourself in the mirror every day, but do you really notice yourself? Try answering the following questions.

1. Which is higher, your right eyebrow or your left?

2. Sketch your hairline on a piece of paper.

3. Without taking your shoes off, tell which is longer—your big toe or your thumb?

4. Is your earlobe attached at the bottom or does it hang free?

5. Is the width of your nose at the nostrils more, the same, or less than the distance from your nose to your top lip?

6. Is the width of your mouth more, the same, or less than the distance between the inside edges of your eyes?

7. If you put the base of your hand (fingers pointing up) even with your chin, the tip of your middle finger would come up to (a) the bridge of your nose; (b) halfway up your forehead; (c) your hairline (or, in the case of those with receding hairlines, where the hair *used* to be).

8. Borrow a hair dye color chart (or clip one from a magazine ad) and identify the color that is closest to your natural hair color.

Answers: Check your answers in a mirror.

Here are some classic observation questions that draw on everyday experiences. They're old but they're still fun . . . and often puzzling.

1. Does Lincoln face left or right on the U.S. penny?

2. Do jar lids unscrew clockwise or counterclockwise?

3. How many fingers does Mickey Mouse have? How many toes?

4. Without looking—does your watch have Arabic or Roman numerals? Does it have all the numbers, or just 12-3-6-9?

5. Which letters of the alphabet don't appear on the telephone buttons or dial?

Answers

1. Right
2. Counterclockwise
3. Three fingers and a thumb; his feet are always covered by shoes.
4. (Look)
5. Q and Z

A VISUALIZING EXERCISE

Glance at a three-letter or four-letter word on a sign, on television, or in a newspaper. Shut your eyes and fix the word on the blackboard of your mind. When you can see it clearly, spell it backward. As soon as this becomes easy to do, use longer and longer words.

A LISTENING EXERCISE

Have someone read you a sentence from a newspaper or book, or listen to a sentence on the radio or TV. Turn the sound down immediately and fix the sentence in your mind. Then say it backwards to yourself. Start with short sentences and work up. (It may help to "write" the sentence on a mental blackboard so you can "read" it backward.)

SOLVING PROBLEMS
AND MAKING
DECISIONS

Problem solving and decision making aren't always the same thing. Rescuing a cat from a tree (problem) is different from naming it (decision). But the two processes frequently overlap and both use the same initial stages of collecting and evaluating information. Both use a committee of the parts of the mind to reach resolution. And both require Executive approval to be carried out.

> Solving a problem or making a decision is easy. All it takes is rational logic, and man is, above all things, a rational animal. (*If you believe anything in the above statement, I have some nice swampland in Florida I'd like to sell you!*)

Man is gloriously illogical, basing solutions and decisions on the needs and input of all parts of the mind, filtered through a lifetime accumulation of *Manual of Procedures* "rules." This haphazard, round table process is "bad" only when the result seems faulty or the process itself produces confusion and anxiety. Yet, there is a lot of concern about "bad" decisions and solutions.

Newsweek magazine reports that studies at the Center for Decision Research at the University of Chicago Graduate School of Business show that "most people are woefully muddled information processors who often stumble along ill-chosen shortcuts to reach bad conclusions." The Princeton-based multinational development firm of Kepner-Tregoe, founded by two social scientists, Charles H. Kepner and Benjamin B. Tregoe, authors of the landmark book *The New Rational Manager*, estimates that U.S. companies use "good decision skills" only about 12 percent of the time.

But what proportion of the decisions made or problems solved with "good skills" turned out well? How does that percentage compare with the results of decisions and solutions made with "poor" skills? As every manager or parent of small children knows, sometimes it doesn't matter *what* decision is made or solution proposed, as long as *something* happens so that people can go forward.

LOGIC

In our age, logic is king. Yet many women routinely and painfully remove hair from their eyebrows while tediously gluing hair to their eyelids. Before you mutter something about the inconsistency of women, consider the average western male who will spend thousands of hours removing hair from the lower portion of his face and thousands of dollars restoring hair to the upper portion through hair tonics, transplants, and toupees.

On a more serious (or grimly humorous) level, most people hold strong opinions on abortion and the death penalty. Not too logically, those who favor one frequently oppose the other. Somewhat defensively, they will come up with "logical" explanations for this inconsistency. For instance, people who favor the death penalty often say it is a deterrent to crime, despite numerous studies showing otherwise. Similarly, those who oppose capital punishment probably wouldn't change their minds if new studies showed that it dramatically reduced crime. People's decisions—their beliefs—are obviously based on factors far more complex than "logic."

But logic is essential for solving problems and making decisions. Nearly all of us develop our own inborn ability to evaluate personal experiences: If I put my hand in the fire, it gets burned. But the more sophisticated structuring method that has come down to us in fits and starts through thinkers like Aristotle and Descartes must be learned.

This structuring is sometimes called "logic" and sometimes "critical thinking"—there is some argument about the distinction. For our purposes, we'll say that logic is an inborn *ability*, but we must learn the *skill* of critical thinking.

Critical thinking combines knowledge, skepticism, and analytic techniques. We learn to make inferences and deductions, to sequence, compare, sort, collect, and discard, as well as to interpret and evaluate arguments. "Experts solve problems," says psychologist Roger Peters, "not by brute force or sheer computational power, but by applying all kinds of highly organized information." To be useful, critical thinking must usually be followed by action. (One current test of logical thinking is the Watson-Glaser Critical Thinking Appraisal; surprisingly, says Peters, people with high IQs often get low marks on this test.)

PROCESSING INFORMATION

"Brains, like computers, are not 'user-friendly,'" says psychologist Richard Bandler. "They do exactly what they're *told* to do, not what you *want* them to do. Then you get mad at them because they don't do what you *meant* to tell them to do!" Often this confusion comes from mixed messages. The millions of bits of information that we feed our brains daily get sorted in a variety of ways by each part of our mind, and these different colorings affect our evaluation.

Framing. All information is presented and evaluated in some context, frequently linguistic. A vague, inaccurate, or subtly manipulative "framing" might have a serious influence on the answer you come up with. In a University of Chicago experiment with the language of framing, *Newsweek* magazine reports, one group was told that a hypothetical business venture had an 80 percent chance of success. Most of that group voted to try it. Another group was told there was a 20 percent risk of failure, and most decided against it.

The first step in evaluating information is to frame it. What are you comparing to what? Advertisers and politicians are especially adept at getting you off track. For example, a toaster oven is advertised as more energy efficient than any other toaster oven. But is the toaster oven more or less efficient than a regular oven, a toaster, or a microwave oven? A senator brags that he has sponsored more tax legislation. Than whom? Of what kind? A toothpaste or shaving cream contains more factor X than any other toothpaste or shaving cream on the market. But how much factor X do you actually need? And are there other (and better) sources?

We've already talked about framing as a tool for setting goals and enjoying each part of your life. It's also valuable for evaluating the negative parts. With proper framing, you can see criticisms and complaints as valuable information rather than petty annoyances or crushing blows. Thomas Edison did not regard each of his 6,000 futile attempts to find a filament for the incandescent light bulb as another failure. Instead he realized that he had eliminated yet another substance that wouldn't work. Each failure put him one step closer to the correct solution.

Sloppy labeling prevents accurate framing. This may be the most potent argument against profanity. When you label a person or situation as an "expletive deleted," you no longer have to respond to the real person or problem and all its potential. In wartime, the enemy is quickly assigned an insulting communal nickname. It's much easier to kill a "gook" or a "Hun" than a fiddle player with a warm sense of humor who loves flowers and dogs.

Immediacy. Our natural bias favors the first available information: "My mind is made up, don't bother me with facts." After we have absorbed enough information to form a strong picture, we get confused by new information and reject it. It is irrelevant. It is annoying. It is even threatening. (Imagine yourself as Galileo, announcing that the earth goes around the sun when every existing institution has based its authority on the earth being the center of the universe!)

Just as a hometown car crash rates more newspaper space than a major disaster in Tibet, we tend to let one piece of immediate, personal information outweigh a quantity of information from a distance:

"My brother-in-law tried to start his own business and it was a disaster."

(*Future Rosy for New Small Businesses Says National Advisor.*)

"Sue always flies Sky-High Airlines and they've never lost her luggage."
(*Sky-High Leader in Lost Luggage, Study Shows.*)

"We're going to buy another Gopher-8 station wagon because our last one gave us such good service."
(*Recall of All Gopher-8s Ordered—Major Defects Cited.*)

We tend to accept the most immediately available information, especially if it fits in with our preconceptions. It takes real stamina to dig further, prepared to reconsider, when we already "know everything."

Tradition. Repeating past behavior is both an imperative and a booby trap. Did it work last time? Then do it again. Is this situation or person similar to another one? Then respond in the same way. Much of the time this works. The trick is to recognize that you are doing this and that flexibility is as important as consistency. (Emerson said, "A foolish consistency is the hobgoblin of little minds. . . . ")

Prejudging provides a valuable framework for filing future information. Our *Manual of Procedures* saves us lots of time and energy because it saves reevaluating every bit of information: "I don't spit at people. I put my socks on first, then my shoes." But it also gets cluttered up with ideas that need to be reconsidered periodically: "Never talk to strangers." "All Democrats are stupid jerks." Some of the data in our *Manual* under "Beliefs" can be conflicting and even dangerous. "Beliefs," says psychologist Richard Bandler, "can compel perfectly nice people to go out and kill other human beings for an idea, and even feel good about it. . . ."

Evaluating. False logic can be a lot of fun. For instance, all opera singers have two feet; I have two feet; therefore I am an opera singer. Or, most teenagers listen to rock music; most teenagers have cavities; therefore rock music causes cavities.

This seems amusing until we get into some of the reasoning behind major social and political decisions. Such reasoning is especially hard to spot and debunk when it supports our natural biases and beliefs.

Let's say, for example, that in Guzzle County 70 percent of the drivers involved in accidents have a blood-alcohol level of 2.0, well above intoxication. Most of us would conclude that drunk drivers cause accidents. But that is backward logic. It would first be necessary to get similar statistics for the drivers who *don't* have accidents. If, in this unique case, 90 percent of them are also intoxicated, then we would have to conclude that in Guzzle County drunk drivers are less likely to have accidents than sober ones. But few of us would insist on the additional information. The first interpretation fits our preconceived belief.

Or let's say that 75 percent (an imaginary statistic) of the people arrested for sex crimes are found to have sexually explicit magazines in their homes. Did the magazines cause their criminal behavior? Or reflect their aberration? Before you reply, look at the same premise using different information. Suppose that further studies show that 85 percent of those arrested have milk in their refrigerators. Did the milk cause their criminal behavior? Or was it a symptom of their problems? To reach a more valid conclusion, you would need to compare the amount of sexually explicit literature in the homes of accused sex criminals with the amount in the homes of the general noncriminal population.

Backward logic *is* necessary in some cases when the problem is the result of an unknown cause—for instance, identifying the source of an epidemic. Then you start with the result—a hundred people with ptomaine—and gather information which hopefully will lead you back to a common cause of their illness. But use backward logic wisely. It's very seductive and can trip you up.

When you use figures, ratios, or comparisons in reaching a conclusion, be sure that you are not being tricked by false or sloppy inferences or inappropriate backward logic. Before accepting anyone else's reasoning, play Sherlock Holmes and come up with as many alternate explanations as possible. If the logic withstands the test, then your conclusion will have a better chance of being correct.

Changing Gears. Have several different gears for problem solving. First, survey the problem at cruise speed. Use rapid, intuitive, holistic thinking. Don't knock intuition. It is "not the opposite of rationality," says Daniel Isenberg of the Harvard Business School, as reported in the *Harvard Business Review.* "Nor is it a random process of guessing. Rather, it is based on extensive experience both in analysis and problem solving and in implementation, and, to the extent that the lessons of experience are logical and well-founded, then so is the intuition." Obviously intuition involves contributions from all the aspects of the mind.

Once you have an overview, drop down into first gear. Use analytic, systematic, and linear thinking, all the skills of your Organizing Mind and Knowing Mind, to go over details. This is where you make charts and lists and sketches.

The combination of the high and low gears is essential for major problem solving. The insight necessary to unlock the secret of Egyptian hieroglyphics or of the double helix may have come in a unique burst of inspiration, but the low gears are crucial to completing the concept.

Questioning. Ask stupid questions. Dare to be dumb. Czech novelist Milan Kundera says, "The stupidity of people comes from having an answer for everything. The wisdom of the novel comes from having a question for everything." He was speaking of literature, but the same applies to life. When we are young, we are ashamed to "show our ignorance," and so pass up brilliant opportunities for discovery. Most people are delighted to explain something they care about to another person. The next time someone mentions something you've never heard of, *ask*. Watch him glow. Even if you occasionally run into an insecure soul who stares at you incredulously and laughs, laugh with him. You are dealing with a fragile ego, and your open, unabashed, "I never knew that! Tell me about it," will be the highlight of his day.

PROBLEM SOLVING

Wally says: "I'm never able to solve anything. There are so many things to consider and one answer just creates a lot more questions. I never get out from under and I give up."

Wally's friends have resigned themselves to his constant air of being overwhelmed with problems. At lunch, he tells Frank about his latest dilemma: he has been offered a substantial raise if he will take on a risky assignment that would require him to move to another state. "Great," says Frank. "No, not great," says Wally gloomily. And he raises a series of issues. What if the project fails and he ends up getting fired? What if he can't find an appropriate place to live in the new city that will take his three Irish setters? What will he do for friends? What if he can't sublet his apartment and loses it? What about his retirement plan if he fails? What about his elderly mother who lives near him now? Who will look after her and what if she gets sick? And if she should move to the new city, the climate would be terrible for her health and she would miss her friends.

Frank offers some encouraging solutions to all of Wally's problems, but Wally shoots each of them down. "Well," says Frank finally, "I guess you shouldn't accept."

"What do you mean, don't accept?" cries Wally. "My whole future depends on this! If I don't take it, I won't be considered for another promotion. I'll be washed up before I'm thirty. McGillicudy will see that I'm eased out of the company. I'll have to take a salary cut or lose my job. I won't be able to afford my great apartment. My dogs and I will be out in the street. And my mother will die of shame!"

Frank is now overwhelmed too. He thought he was offering helpful suggestions to a friend. Instead, he was supporting Wally's game of "See, there's no solution!" Wally was getting a lot of attention and strokes for his inability to see a way out of his problems. Now, there *are* situations where the ability to delay action is valuable—while waiting for sufficient information or weighing the emotional impact of a "logical" action (or the impact of logic on an emotional action). A few people can even function successfully without ever resolving anything, just letting others act for them. They carry the expression "that's *his* problem" to its ultimate. But most of us need and enjoy using our problem-solving abilities.

> Gordon says: "I'm always jumping to conclusions.
> Then I find I was wrong."

A vigorous curiosity can get just a few bits of information before it fills in the rest of the picture and reports it as facts ready for action. This is essential. Without this unique ability, we would be hard-pressed to walk down a staircase, read a sentence, or follow a conversation.

But sometimes this genius at filling in the blanks uses the

wrong information. Like one of the blind men in the Indian fable, it grabs hold of an elephant's trunk or ear and infers that all of the elephant is exactly the same.

The great strength of our mind is that the same part that knows how to learn also knows how to play. We can *learn* to wait for more information before reporting. We can make a deliberate game of waiting, something like "Simon Says." If you frequently act on incomplete information and want to change, get in touch with your sense of play. Intrigue yourself with the possibility of working on a larger puzzle by waiting for more pieces to work with.

In 1958, the two social scientists Charles H. Kepner and Benjamin B. Tregoe started a company designed to show corporations how to solve problems and make decisions. Their book *The New Rational Manager* describes a series of steps for analyzing problems, decisions, performance, and management. The steps were so simple, logical, and workable, that the processes have become standard for hundreds of businesses and more than a million managers and employees. Kepner-Tregoe problem-solving techniques are primarily intended for tracking down a malfunction in a complex piece of machinery or production process or for resolving manpower problems, but the steps can also be applied to many everyday puzzles.

When something goes wrong, most people ask, "Why?" or—almost as likely—"Whose *fault* is it?" People, businesses, and governments spend a lot of energy assigning blame. Kepner-Tregoe approaches problems from a completely different angle. Vastly oversimplified, a portion of their problem-solving technique goes like this: When a problem occurs, don't ask *why*. Instead, start by identifying the problem. (It may not be what you think it is!) Ask when, where, what, how, what is different between the time there was no problem and the time there was, between the usable product and the defective product, between the place where the problem is and the place where it isn't. What is the deviation pattern? Often there are several differences which may account for the problem, alone or in combination.

A common result of this questioning is that the problem gets restated. "That stupid Joe is always late with his reports," could become "Joe has a bigger workload than anyone else," or "Joe isn't notified about deadlines," or even "Joe's secretary has been out sick."

One disturbing Kepner-Tregoe case history concerned a woman who was promoted to a more demanding job within an insurance company. Very quickly, her new department manager realized that she was a "problem." Although her workstation had just been redecorated to improve morale and efficiency, the new employee made too many mistakes—10 percent compared to the department average of 1 percent. Also, she didn't socialize with the others and complained constantly of headaches. Her attitude seemed questionable. She was counseled repeatedly, given warnings about her job performance, and asked to improve. Finally she was demoted and sent to another department.

An experienced department member moved over to the empty workstation. The errors continued. This time the company decided it was a mechanical problem. The equipment was checked thoroughly, but no malfunction could be discovered. By now, a committee was working on the problem. Finally they applied the Kepner-Tregoe process of looking for all deviations. They discovered that the errors occurred *only* at that workstation and *only* on sunny days. Sun did not affect any other stations. And what else was different about that workstation? Well, it was right next to the windows—the windows which had gotten new sheer curtains just before the unfortunate new employee joined the department. The sun reflected on the screen, causing errors and also causing headaches.

The disturbing part of this case history, presented by Kepner-Tregoe from the company's viewpoint, is that the woman was not told about the solution and offered the option of returning to her job: "The company felt that it was 'too embarrassing'..." The company saved face, but the woman will go through life believing she doesn't have the ability for this higher-level job. Most of the Kepner-Tregoe stories, however, have much more satisfying conclusions. They stress logical steps for identifying a problem and arriving at a workable solution.

Problem solving can require meticulous calculations or it can be the result of the proverbial light bulb going on. Often we need to turn a problem upside down to see it a new way. People have pinned their clothes together since prehistoric times, but the safety pin is barely a century old. Envelopes, toothpaste in tubes, and frozen dinners are all recent solutions to problems that no one knew they had. In fact the best way to get rich is to invent a problem—yellow waxy buildup, tired blood, woofer wobble, cellulite—and then offer a pricey cure for it.

MAKING DECISIONS

Decision making is a group effort by all parts of the mind. The knowing part provides raw data. The organizing part evaluates it. The wondering part offers solutions and the organizing part compares these with past successes and failures. Then they all report to the executive part for a resolution. The one factor that routinely gets snubbed in this process is the emotions. This is the part of the mind most likely to sabotage a decision that it has not participated in.

Emotions often take a bad rap:

> Where passion rules,
> How weak does reason prove.
> —John Dryden

But when there are decisions requiring changes, there are often emotions. Ask yourself how you feel. Trust yourself enough to acknowledge and respond to your own feelings.

Sam was a corporate president who was really stuck. Consultants had advised that his company would make more money if it moved to another state. They presented charts, statistics, projections. He resisted. They went back and checked their figures. Again he resisted. They researched case histories of similar moves to that state. Still he resisted. Finally they pressed him for his reasons. He offered a number of weak excuses, but was too ashamed to tell them the real reason which he confided to a colleague of mine: he didn't want to leave the house his parents and grandparents had lived in and where he and his wife had raised their children before she died.

If this sounds frivolous, consider the results of a survey of businesses that moved out of New York City to the suburbs during the late 1960s. The study, as reported in the *New York Times,* disclosed that 85 percent of firms moved to within five miles of the home of the Chief Executive Officer!

It is clear that no decision can be completely free of personal considerations. In the real world, we use nonrational methods to simplify complex problems. Ideally, when we sit down to make a major decision, we draw up charts, make lists of pros and cons, research alternative actions, meditate, get advice, perhaps draw models of possible outcomes. But the world is rarely ideal. The most important decisions of our life—buying a car, going to college, getting married—are often made on sheer adrenaline. If they turn out okay, then it was a "smart move" and, with hindsight, we congratulate ourselves for our wisdom. If they go sour, we blame the result on the lack of proper planning and come up with explanations for the momentary lapse in our judgment. (Comedian Stan Laurel recalled that he married one of his numerous wives because they lacked enough money to rent separate rooms during a vaudeville tour.)

What is a successful decision? Is it one that achieves the result you think you want? Or one that makes you feel good about yourself and the situation? Or one that, in the context of time, provides the most positive results? Obviously evaluating a decision after the fact is as complex as making it.

Once my roof was leaking. I got an estimate for a new roof from a reliable local contractor who had already done some very satisfactory work on my house. But I decided to use a nationally known company, even though their price was higher. My reasoning went like this: "Suppose the small local company isn't around in a few years to stand behind their work. The national company is famous for reliability and has been in business for over a hundred years. I'd better go with them, pay more now, and be sure of a good job and a guarantee." The national company put a handsome new roof on my house.

The next time it rained, my bedroom looked like Niagara Falls. Papers, clothes, books, paintings—all destroyed. It took several years, much expense, and even more aggravation before a court decided that the national company had sold me only boxes of shingles, not a roof. They had fulfilled their obligation by delivering these shingles to a *subcontractor* wearing their uniform, a gentleman who had long since vanished. It took four years and almost three times the original estimated cost before I finally had a roof that didn't leak. (The national company spent considerably more on lawyers than it would have cost them to replace the roof; their rationale was probably that they were establishing legal precedents to protect them from future lawsuits.)

My original decision had been a valid one, based on sound reasoning. The outcome was sheer hell! No wonder tossing a coin is so popular.

Usually a decision involves choosing between two or more things:

1. To act

2. Not to act—to do nothing

or:

1. Yes

2. No

or:

1. To do this

2. To do that

How do you decide? You've made the usual lists of pros and cons, of potential risks and rewards, and still you're undecided. Or you've made up your mind, but you don't carry out your plan. What's wrong?

It's time to try a different approach, consulting each part of your mind. Consider how each responds to the issue. Identify any areas of conflict and resolve them. Otherwise, despite all logic and analysis, the solution may become the real problem.

I have a big blackboard in my office and sometimes I work through a chart such as the one shown on the opposite page with clients who are on the proverbial horns of a dilemma. The lists for Sam, the executive who couldn't decide about moving his company, looked something like this:

Shall We Move the Company to Another State?		
	For	**Against**
Executive Part	Excellent opportunity. Figures support move.	Expense, disruption. (Temporary, offset by future gains)
Wondering Part	Love a challenge. Exciting, different.	Is small-town life for me? Am I too old to adapt?
Organizing Part	Figures seem valid.	Some difficulties. Possibility of $ loss.
Reacting Part	—	*Home*
Knowing Part	I think I can handle the details and changes.	—

Sam was aware enough to know what was blocking his decision. Often we are not. Creating a chart like this can let hidden agendas pop out so they can be dealt with. In Sam's case, he decided that his priority was to not leave his ancestral home. He then had a new set of choices: block the move, authorize the move but stay put at a "home office," change position within the company and operate a "field office," acknowledge that the move is the best step and leave the company. One decision had produced the need for more subdecisions. That's life.

WHEN THE SOLUTION IS THE PROBLEM

Need to organize your drawers? Start. Spending too much money? Stop. Often solutions are easy but carrying them out is hard. When this happens, run the solution through your mind, using the same chart. Find out which parts of your mind have problems in following through with the new way of doing things. Leave the list on the refrigerator or bathroom mirror for several days and add any ideas that strike you. Then see if you can persuade your dissident minds to "change their mind." Cajole them. Dazzle them. Bribe them if necessary. In extreme cases, lie to them. Get them all on the side of the solution so you can go forth as a united front.

No matter how wisely or carefully you decide, you are bound to agonize about some of your choices. The turmoil of facing a decision is nothing compared to the anxiety and regret that some people choose to experience after they have finally made up their minds. If you find yourself deadlocked, dubious, despairing, choose one of the following options:

> I can do it and feel good.
> I can do it and feel miserable.
> I can not do it and feel good.
> I can not do it and feel miserable.

INTUITIVE SOLUTIONS

Often solving a problem requires looking at it in an unusual way: Growing tougher tomatoes instead of manufacturing gentler picking machines, staggered work hours instead of bigger parking lots. (When a chorus lady's towering headdress was too tall to pass through an onstage door, Florenz Ziegfeld ordered the archway made higher.) You've probably read the standard puzzlers about getting a too-tall truck out of a tunnel (let some air out of the tires) or replacing a flat tire when all the nuts have rolled down a grate (borrow one nut from each of the other wheels).

Back on page 47 there was a puzzler about crossing a river with a fox, a goose, and a bag of grain. (You have access to a small boat, operated by pulling a rope from either shore, which will hold only two items at a time. You cannot leave the fox alone with the goose or he will eat it. You cannot leave the goose alone with the grain or she will eat it.) It took four intricate round-trips to get you and your items on the opposite shore uneaten so you could go on your way.

Try to brainstorm some less conventional solutions to this traditional problem. Here are some that people in my workshops have come up with. Some ignore the limitations of the problem and/or the proposed resolution.

- Don't cross the river. (Zero trips)

- Find a bridge. (One trip)

- Find a bigger boat. (One trip)

- Feed the grain to the goose, eat the goose, and then cross with the fox. Technically all the items are then crossing the river. (One trip)

- Spread the loose grain in the bottom of the boat, seat the fox, and make the goose swim along behind. (One trip)

- Put the grain in the boat, leash the fox on one side of the boat and the goose on the other and make them both swim. (One trip)

Try to come up with at least three more solutions.

PRACTICAL SOLUTIONS

Find the next number in each of the following sequences.

1. 1, 2, 3, 4, 5, 6, 7, 8, _____

2. 1, 3, 5, 7, 9, 11, _____

3. 5, 10, 15, 20, _____

4. 1, 4, 7, 10, 13, 16, 19, _____

5. 1, 2, 4, 7, 11, 16, 22, _____

6. The famous Fibonacci Sequence (really very easy if you relax): 1, 1, 2, 3, 5, 8, 13, 21, 34, _____

7. A phone number sequence: 428-6339, 286-3394, 863-3942, 633-9428, _____

8. And my favorite. This one is tricky because it requires some general knowledge: 14, 18, 23, 34, 42, 50, 59, _____

9. How about this verbal sequence: MN NO OP PQ QR _____

10. Too easy? Try this one and those that follow: allegra, barb, cynic, did, fluff, _____

11. adverb, basic, card, done, elf, _____

12. Every young girl loves some exciting _____.

Answers

1. 9 - counting by ones
2. 13 - counting by odd numbers
3. 25 - counting by fives
4. 22 - counting by threes
5. 29 (22 plus 7) Add 1, 2, 3, 4, 5, 6, etc. consecutively to the previous answer:

1	2	4	7	11	16	22
+1	+2	+3	+4	+5	+6	+7
2	4	7	11	16	22	29

(This is a variation on the classic "pyramid numbers," which go 1, 3, 6, 10, 15, 21, 28, 36...)

6. 55 (21 + 34) Fibonacci's sequence adds each number to the previous number to produce the new number.

7. 339-4286 (numbers are rotated)

8. 66th Street, Lincoln Center—the next stop on the west side IRT subway in Manhattan

9. RS

10. gag, giving, gong—any word starting and ending with *g*

11. fig, fog, flying—any word starting with *f* and ending with *g*

12. games, gingersnap—any word starting with *g* (the last letter of each word becomes the first letter of the next word)

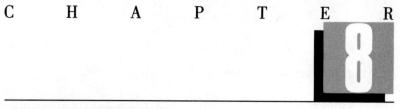

CREATING

Jerry says: "I have to keep coming up with new sales campaign ideas at work, and I'm just burned out."

Ann says: "Everyone in my family is so creative. When they're all talking, I'd like to impress them with my ideas, but I just go blank."

Arthur says: "I'd like to write, or paint, or something like that, but when I do, it isn't any good. I guess I'm just not creative."

Creativity doesn't always mean painting a picture or designing a skyscraper. It can mean putting the pieces of your life together in new, more productive ways.

Creativity is about making connections that haven't been made before in quite the same way. Creativity is about seeing things from a different angle so that you go "Aha!" Creativity is about reframing your interpretation of the events of your life so you can go forward positively and productively. The part of your mind that does all this most effectively is the wondering part.

When you want to unleash your creativity, you need to notice what the rest of your mind is up to. You need to strike a bargain with your otherwise valuable critical executive voice to keep its mouth shut. If you don't, it lurks in the background muttering, "That's not good enough."

Suspending judgment isn't always easy, especially after a life-time of trusting its directives, but it's essential for creativity. Say, "Thank you very much, critical sense, for your interest. Now go for a walk, and when I'm through wondering and exploring and creating and fantasizing, I'll invite you in to critique the result." (It doesn't pay to offend this essential but sometimes cranky part of your mind.)

In the initial stages of creativity, critical judgment is the one thing you *must* send out for sandwiches. Its constant peering over your shoulder, poking and pointing out mistakes, will distract and inhibit you until nothing you do looks good. This enforced vacation can last a few seconds or a few years—whatever time you need to come up with the raw material. Then judgment takes over, evaluat-ing and refining your discoveries.

Anne in the case above could never think of something clever to say at the right moment. This is such a common occurrence that the French have a phrase for it: *l'esprit d'escalier,* literally "the inspira-tion of the staircase," the ideas that come to you too late as you are going out the door. However, Anne had another problem. She was eager to impress people.

This is probably the biggest block there is to being truly creative. I work with a lot of people who have "blocked" themselves creatively and I usually start by asking them why they want to do whatever it is that seems blocked. If they reply "to be important," "to get recognition," "to show so-and-so I can do it," I know the chances of successful therapy are considerably reduced. Their antic-ipated satisfaction comes not from what *they* wish to do but from how they hope *other people* will see them. Their "product" is not the work they create but other people's reactions to it and to them. That's counting on others to supply their pleasure, a heavy and unrealistic responsibility.

This doesn't mean that we don't need support and praise for our creative efforts. Being creative frequently means taking a risk, mak-ing ourselves vulnerable, and we can use all the protection and strokes we can get. But recognition is the fertilizer, not the fruit, of creativity.

Only a very few, totally dedicated people can do creative work in a relative vacuum, never caring what anyone else thinks. One example of this rare type of human is plant geneticist Barbara McClintock. For half a century her colleagues totally ignored her attempts to prove that genes could "jump" from one place to another on a chromosome. Yet when she received the Nobel prize for medicine at age 81, her work was called "one of the two greatest discoveries of our times in genetics." McClintock commented, "When you know you're right, you don't care what others think."

But support helps. Lyricist Marshall Barer recalls the weeks before his hit musical *Once Upon a Mattress* opened in 1959. The role of the princess who encountered the pea was originally written for feisty, wisecracking, little Nancy Walker but then recast with a tall, gawky, unsophisticated newcomer, Carol Burnett. Naturally many of the songs for street-smart Walker had to be discarded and new ones written for Burnett. Days before opening they still lacked one of the crucial songs, traditionally called the "11:00 spot" because it's the last big number before the finale. Barer wrote lyric after lyric and composer Mary Rogers set many of them to music, but none of them seemed right.

A few days before opening, still without a number, Barer and Burnett stood in the rain in front of the Phoenix Theatre, trying to get a cab. "She turned to me," recalls Barer, "and said, 'Marshall, even if there's no second act, if everyone gets up and goes home after the first act curtain, I'll still feel that I was in one hell of a show.' I was so buoyed I went home and wrote the lyrics for 'Happily Ever After' which stopped the show. Several years later, when a similar problem arose on another show, the leading lady [also a popular TV performer] looked me in the eye and said grimly, 'You're supposed to be a comedy writer. *Make me funny.* ' Nothing can shrivel you faster than being ordered to be funny. The show was a flop." Someone believing in you can sure make a difference, even in a seasoned professional.

THE TWO-PART CREATIVE PROCESS

Creativity is a two-part process. In each part, different parts of your mind need to take charge. Outside instructions can give directions

—"A better mouse trap, please." "How about some pictures on the ceiling, Michelangelo?"—but they can never order results. These restricting outside voices can even include that of your own mental executive. When you give yourself messages like "Be more clever," or "Be more creative," the organizing part of your mind, something of a toady, jumps to obey the command and ends up blocking the process instead. It's something like handling a governmental requisition in octuplicate requesting aesthetically acceptable graphics on a vertical cellulose inscribing surface produced manually by a carbon distributing drafting device—in other words, a pencil drawing. Turn off these outside voices, your own included, while you use this two-part process:

Part One: The Exploratory Phase. You brainstorm, toss out any silly idea, write or say or draw anything that comes into your head, bounce ideas around, try things backwards, play games, dance, sing, stand on your head, play "what if . . . ," draw inspiration without any restrictions.

Part Two: The Crafting Phase. You go back over what you have produced, choosing what's good, what works, what pleases you. Then the organizing part of your mind does what it does best—it organizes and polishes what you have done.

WHAT IS IMAGINATION?

There's a popular notion that children and the less-sophisticated have more imagination than the rest of us. American drama critic Clayton Hamilton expressed a different view in his book *Studies in Stagecraft:*

> . . . the supernatural is immeasurably easier, both to
> fabricate and to appreciate, than is the natural
> . . . because it requires less maturity of imagination.
> Imagination is the faculty for realization. Contrary to
> common belief, children are, as a rule, incapable of
> imagination. They tell themselves stories of ghosts
> and goblins and fairies because they are unable to
> realize men and women and children; they invent
> exceptions to the laws of life because they cannot

> understand the law. . . . It has required a more
> matured imagination to perceive that divinity is
> evidenced not in . . . some willful illegality of nature,
> but in law itself, majestic and immutable.

This is a startling view indeed, challenging some of our age-old beliefs about the creative process, but it is worth pondering, if only to give you new respect for the powers of your mind. A few hundred years ago, the most sophisticated human mind could not imagine the circulation of the blood or the orbits of the planets or the existence of the atom. A few hundred years from now, our descendants will wonder at our lack of imagination in failing to perceive the everyday facts of their existence.

The organizing part of your mind makes order out of our world by discarding information that doesn't fit its model of reality. Then the wondering part rushes to fill in the gaps. It can do this by providing boogeymen and magic spells to explain the unexplainable. But how much richer and more imaginative if you set about exploring the reasons for the gaps, if you set about conceiving a circulatory system or a solar system.

The moral is: Never dismiss the creative abilities of your mind as "just imagination," for, at its strongest, your mind holds the capacity to conceive of the universe.

IMAGERY

Children *do* sometimes come up with dazzling insights and images. Because they have less framework for comparing and evaluating information, they must sequence and match up the bits randomly until something clicks. It's a highly inefficient method, but one that occasionally produces a startling innovation, something like computer-written poetry. But children are unaware of their own brilliance. It takes a mind with more structures, more techniques, more knowledge, to recognize these pearls from the mouths of babes.

Visual images are important to many kinds of creativity— designing, painting, planning, even dancing. Although writing is a verbal art, successful writers turn the visual images in their minds into words that can be transformed back into visual images by the reader, something like a voice traveling as electronic pulses over a telephone wire before becoming a voice again.

Using visual imagery to overcome illness, a poor golf score, lack of confidence, or even lack of money is a popular technique and in some cases quite effective. All the visualizing in the world can't make you richer or make an empty taxi appear where none exists. But visualizing plus intelligence *can* make you more alert to the subtle signs of opportunities for increased income or for getting a taxi.

Even without special training programs, most of us use visualization consciously all the time. We arrange ourselves just so in front of a mirror and then go forth, confident that we know what we look like to others. We picture our lunch so strongly that we start salivating at 11:00 A.M. We think about an absent loved one and experience a rush of images.

This ability to see with the mind is partly inborn, partly developed by training. It is a valuable skill, essential for many careers. Psychologist Richard Bandler notes that with the ability to make vivid mental images " . . . you can learn how to be a civil engineer or a psychotic. One pays better than the other, but it's not as much fun." Even if you choose less demanding applications, visualization can be a constant source of intense personal pleasure, letting you re-experience beauty, excitement, grandeur, contentment at will.

YOU'VE GOT TO BE CRAZY

Bandler's comment pokes fun at one of the popular myths—that you have to be crazy to be creative. Seventeenth century poet John Dryden wrote, "Great wits are sure to madness near allied, and thin partitions do their bounds divide."

There are two reasons for this legend:

1. The reactions of the individual to creative thinking.

2. The reactions of society to the creative person.

First—for the individual, the creative process requires the temporary suspension of most of the rules, turning off traditions, dogma, much of the contents of the *Manual of Procedures.* This is a heady experience and causes some folks to question the "rules" in other areas of their lives—a highly unpopular activity in tightly organized or repressive societies. Some folks confuse eccentricity with creativity and reverse the process, adopting what they see as the trappings of creativity—oddball clothes, attitudes, and manners—in the hope that insight and inspiration will follow. It's understandable that people passionate about order may block their own natural creativity because they see it as part of a larger, disturbing, and disruptive package.

Second—the reactions of society to the creative person. Although societies need and often decree creativity, they are always suspicious of the process. "Creativity demands independence; organizations demand conformity. . . . " note Michael Ray and Rochelle Myers of Stanford University's Graduate School of Business. And "Creativity is threatening in the same way madness is," says cognitive psychologist Roger Peters, "because it is by nature unpredictable." Obviously society can be ambivalent about its own life force.

PROCESS AND PRODUCT

"There are two kinds of people in the world," says artist/product designer Jean Ray Laury, "Process People and Product People." Fortunately, she points out, most of us are a little of both.

Process People, says Laury, will work hard on something for hours or weeks or years and then happily dump the results in the wastebasket. They have taught themselves a *process* which they will use for the rest of their lives. Product People, on the other hand, need to have visible results for every effort. For them, effort without evidence of it is effort wasted.

Pure Process People can find it hard to finish every project. Their curiosity carries them on to the next activity with little input from the organizing part of their mind. They are *mission-oriented.*

Pure Product People resent any time spent learning and exploring, and may measure their own worth by how much they produce. They are constantly evaluating what they do, often ignoring important emotional messages. They are *goal-oriented*.

Obviously a balance is most productive, using the approach that suits the project at hand. But if you have to choose, go for process. What if there is no gratification at the end of a long struggle? If you enjoyed the journey itself—the process—then you can survive lots of disappointments at the end. Suppose you spend grueling years becoming a doctor or accountant or astronaut and then discover that you want to do something else. Are those years wasted? Not if you took pleasure in your personal development along the way, if you learned ways to cope with life's situations and found unexpected strengths and insights within yourself and others.

A pure Product Person judges everything by the "bottom line." One woman complained that she had wasted 20 years of her life in the wrong job. Yet she admitted that 19 of those years had been happy and productive. It was only the last year when she began to realize that she was ready for a change. Were those 19 years truly wasted? She was rejecting them as both process *and* product.

THREE ARTISTS

Talent and creativity are not always the same thing. I knew a young painter named Mickey. He was totally devoted to his work, living in an unheated tenement room, taking menial jobs to pay for paints and canvas, scrounging meals, going without medical and dental care. He really suffered so that he could turn out canvas after canvas, literally hundreds each year. I would like to report that the world finally recognized his genius, but sadly it didn't because he had none. His work was totally lacking in originality and technique. It was awful. But Mickey was thoroughly enjoying the *process*. His mission was to be a painter and he succeeded.

At about the same time I knew Mickey, I attended a student opera recital at a prestigious music school. All the singers were very competent, but one stood out, a handsome tenor with a voice of such beauty, power, and intelligence that it raised the hairs on my neck. With tears in my eyes and palms raw from clapping, I was certain he would become one of the major operatic voices of this century.

In that same recital was an awkward, earnest young man with

an unremarkable voice. I told myself that he might make an opera chorus, but surely no more.

Several years later the awkward young man was under contract to a top opera company, doing supporting roles. He had worked incredibly hard and become a reliable, consistent performer with a long career ahead of him in second leads and character roles. As for the brilliant young tenor, I learned through friends that he had stopped singing entirely and taken up a profession that was only marginally legal where, at least, his good looks would bring him lots of adulation and income. There's a moral or two here somewhere. Perhaps it's that each of these people had the talent to create the life he wanted, selecting it from among the gifts he possessed.

LIMITATIONS

Limitations can spur creativity. The Sistine Chapel ceiling was an utterly impossible place to put a painting, full of juts and vaults. Other artists had refused to touch it. Michelangelo was browbeaten into taking the job, but he was creative enough to use its faults to project and define his powerful design. The restrictions defined what he couldn't do, but *he* defined what he *could* do.

Think of the times you had to improvise and you came up with something surprisingly good. Trust yourself to see and use limitations as springboards. If there aren't any limitations and you're totally blank, create some imaginary ones to spur your thinking. When the sight of a blank sheet of paper leaves you just as blank, make up a silly restriction until you get started: "No words starting with *L*," or "Three adjectives in each sentence." After two sentences you'll resent this hindrance to your thoughts and discard it. When you have complete and somewhat frightening freedom to plan something, set temporary limits to get yourself started.

TIPS FROM
THE THREE STOOGES

Humor is essential for creativity. "Any joke that makes you feel good is likely to help you think more broadly and creatively," says

Alice M. Isen, a psychologist at the University of Maryland, as reported in the *San Francisco Examiner*. The elation enlarges your view of the world, making you see many more possibilities than you would if you were in neutral or, worse, depressed. Isen's study, reported in the *Journal of Personality and Social Psychology*, found that people who had watched a short comedy film of television "bloopers" did better on a test requiring creative solutions than people who had watched a film about math or who had exercised. Moral: Be silly.

RONNY ROCK

Remember Johnny Carson's fake toy commercials with "Susy String" and "Sammy Stick?" He would take a simple prop and glamorize it in a caricature of a high-pressure TV sales pitch, showing dozens of imaginative and ridiculous uses to justify its absurd price tag.

Pretend that you are writing a television sketch and must come up with at least twenty uses for "Ronny Rock." To start you off, how about: (1) a doorstop, (2) ballast for canoeing with a 600-pound friend, (3) an end table for Prehistoric Barbie. Keep going.

STRANGE MUSIC

Go to the record collection of a cooperative friend or family member and pull out a record, sight unseen. Play it and respond to the music. Do you want to dance? Dream? Even if it is dreadful, listen for five minutes. Then write down your thoughts and reactions.

(It needs to be someone else's collection because you will come up with preprogrammed responses to your own.)

ALPHABETSOUP

Call a friend and ask him to say any letter of the alphabet. Don't tell him why. Then go to the kitchen and prepare a gourmet dish using at least three foods starting with that letter. No fair shopping. (This is so much fun that you may even get other family members to play, giving you a whole new way to look at the foods you commonly eat: "Okay, honey, it's your turn for Alphabetsoup and your letter is *L*." With *N*, my son came up with Noodles cooked in apricot Nectar and Nutmeg. Yum!)

CAR KEYS

You drop your car keys through a grate just as you finish your shopping and are heading for your car. There they sit, three feet below sidewalk level, glinting at you. In your grocery bag you have:

> 25 feet of clothesline
> 2 AA batteries
> a roll of aluminum foil
> cornflakes
> denture adhesive
> a plastic flyswatter
> 3 refrigerator magnets shaped like daisies
> 3 Ping-Pong balls
> 2 light bulbs
> gardening shears

List as many ways as you can think of in five minutes to get the keys out of the grate, using the contents of your shopping bag.

Some possible ways to retrieve the keys from the grate are:

1. Twist and mold the aluminum foil into a 4-foot hook, supported for its first 18 inches by the handle of the flyswatter. Hook keys.

2. Position the magnets on the light bulb and hold in place with foil at the end of a twisted 4-foot length of foil. Lift keys with magnets.

3. Coat light bulb with denture adhesive and dangle on end of the clothesline.

4. Cut plastic flyswatter paddle into hook shape with shears. Tie clothesline through hang-up hole in swatter handle. Weight paddle with two magnets on opposite sides of paddle. Lower and hook keys.

5. Loop clothesline between blades of shears to hold them in open position and secure to handles. Balance with magnets. Lower shears on clothesline and insert cocked blade of shears through key ring.

6. Double whammy: Unwind a foot or so of the clothesline into two separate strands and tie one battery to each end. Put magnets and denture adhesive on batteries. Lower onto keys, retrieving them by a combination of adhesion and magnetism.

Keep going until you come up with a way to use the cornflakes.

NOSPEAK

You live in a totalitarian society where free speech is forbidden. You encounter other people whom you think would like to talk with you about prohibited subjects. List all the ways you can think of in one minute that you might use to communicate with them so that other people wouldn't suspect.

Some means of secret communication are: sign codes using the hands and body; verbal codes substituting euphemisms for actual subjects; position codes using objects in the room; musical codes, either spelling things out with notes of the scale or with rhythms, such as Morse Code, etc.

BRAVE NEW WORLD

Genetic engineering—gene splicing—has raised intricate social, environmental, and philosophical questions. The technology makes possible a multitude of new organisms. New drugs and medical tests are already on the market, and more is promised: cures for genetic diseases; bugs that will gobble toxic wastes; larger, healthier plants and meat animals; new fuels to replace coal and oil.

According to a story in the *San Francisco Chronicle,* science fiction writer Ray Bradbury is enthusiastic: "There are no pitfalls. . . . Dictators are not going to take over the world and create a race of supermen. That's out of B movies." Biologist Barry Commoner says, "I compare it always with the unhappy experience that we've had with the petrochemical industry." And Harvard historian Everett Mendelsohn warns: "We have to re-pose some of the older questions. . . Toward what end? Controlled by whom? To fulfill what values and at what cost? Who will gain? Who will lose?"

Here are some questions raised by genetic engineering:

• Will human beings be produced in a laboratory? If so, to what end and how will this affect humanity?

• Will food production become so easy and inexpensive that farmers will be bankrupted and forced off their land as the world food market collapses? Or will farmers need to use only a small portion of their land to grow crops and become millionaire entrepreneurs, building housing on the remaining land?

• If food is this plentiful, what will happen to the world's population growth? How will this affect civilization?

• Will the outdoor applications of genetic engineering unwittingly trigger some form of pestilence, such as a plant disease or insect that is immune to any control?

• Gene splicing technology is now within the reach of any bright high school student. Will gene hackers begin to dabble in creating new life forms, just as computer hackers enjoy breaking into national security computers? What could be the consequences?

- Will some nation develop virulent biotoxins for a ghastly new form of germ warfare?

Consider the above and create your prediction of the future of genetic engineering, including realistic ways to regulate and guide its future.

SPEAK UP

Remember Anne back at the beginning of the chapter? She was eager to impress others with her creativity and brilliance but found herself tongue-tied. Some people who "can't think of anything to say" are listening too intently to their own voices to interact with those around them. Anne may be evaluating what she wants to say or considering what is being said around her. She could become so engrossed with a particular comment that she goes off into a trance while the images ricochet around her mind, producing multitudes of internal conversations that block her from noticing subsequent remarks.

Either way, she is not truly listening to what is being said so she probably can't contribute anything bright to the conversation. Anne's assignment is to forget her own attempts at cleverness and to notice and support the cleverness of the people she is with. She will be amazed at how her interest will impress and convince others of her own innate intelligence and sparkling wit. If you think this is easy, challenge yourself to try it the next time you are in a group.

PLAYING CARDS

At the beginning of this chapter, Jerry complained that he was burned out, trying to come up constantly with new ideas for sales campaigns. After all, there are just so many ways to do something. Experts have been announcing for the past ten thousand years that everything has already been written or discovered or invented so there is no point in going further.

If you still need to come up with new material, you might try a trick used by the author of over a hundred scripts for a children's cartoon series about a little boy and his animal friend. He had made up word cards, many of the words having alternate meanings, such as "pen," "wind," or "grate." When the writer ran low on ideas, he would turn to his cards. He would shuffle the cards and deal out three sets of three on the table. It might look like this:

1. race	hidden	duck
2. rope	flee/flea	horn
3. luck	wave	secret

Then he'd try to contrive plots around each sequence. Maybe something like this:

1. race-hidden-duck. Hungry Billy and his dog enter a race whose first prize is a roasted turkey. Just before the finish line, Billy stops to rescue an injured duck and so loses. Billy and dog are sad, but the grateful duck shows them his hidden fishing hole and all ends happily over a fish roast. (Not so hot . . .)

2. rope-flee/flea-horn. Billy and his dog want to join the circus. Billy tries to walk a tightrope and fails, but just then the dog gets fleas and does a wild dance to general applause. Horn is in the circus band. (Possible . . .)

3. luck-wave-secret. Billy finds a secret treasure map, sails on a ship to a desert island, but there is no treasure. Sailing home, a wave washes him overboard and he finds a treasure at the bottom of the sea. Maybe some comical clams and Neptune and a cute dogfish for the dog . . .

Not great stuff, but at least a way to start seeing new options.

NEVER, NEVER, NEVER!

The next time you're totally stuck about something and there doesn't seem to be any way to make it or get it or resolve it, try playing *Never, Never, Never!* Alone or with your coworkers, make statements about what absolutely, positively *won't* work. Really terrible, awful, ridiculous ideas, the worse, the better. This is a real loosener. When you've worked up a list of about 20 things, someone is bound to say, "Hey, wait! That one's not really a bad idea." By going for the negative, you let the positive pop out.

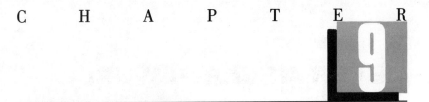

BREAKING
OLD HABITS

I've got to lose this weight, but I can't stay on a diet.

Smoking is killing me, but I just can't quit.

I want to exercise more, but it's so hard to get started.

My husband hates it when I bite my nails, and I promise him I won't, but then I find myself doing it again.

I should keep on top of my personal finances, but it's so easy to let the chore slide. . . .

Bookstores are full of books telling people how to start or stop doing something. They usually offer a gimmick: "Eat only foods starting with *Q*," or "Do these easy aerobics while you sleep." Then the books conclude, " . . . but this won't work unless you *use your will power*."

Fortunately for the income of authors and publishers, pure will power rarely works. This is because "will power" is another name for your mental executive. An order from the top that doesn't take the needs of the other parts of the mind into account is likely to meet with insubordination and rebellion. "Logic" is rarely sufficient to change behavior. "Discipline" is a much-praised but poorly understood concept.

DISCIPLINE

After "love," "sex," "money," and "death," "discipline" may be the most emotion-charged word in the dictionary. There are more than two dozen definitions of the word, including training, drilling, educating, channeling, restricting, chastening, subjugating, and punishing. If you have a somewhat negative view of the word, it is no wonder you are reluctant to develop strategies for getting all of your minds to work together—to be self-channeled, self-*disciplined*.

Being "undisciplined" has even come to be something of a virtue, proof that the individual isn't trapped by dull conventions and authoritarianism. Lack of discipline is seen as liberating, giddy, delightful, even deliciously naughty. As Oscar Wilde quipped, "I can resist everything except temptation."

Perhaps we should replace the term "self-disciplined" with the friendlier one, "self-unified." This avoids the implication that somehow some part of the mind is being forced to do something against its will. Instead it expresses the idea of consensus, wholehearted agreement and cooperation for the good of the body that has kindly consented to carry the mind about.

More than any other challenge, unifying self-discipline requires the consent of every part of the mind. Contemporary author Amy Gross describes discipline as being "extremely gullible and swallowing all the things you tell yourself. It is—by invention, imagination, pledges, lies—arranging your attitude so that as much of yourself as possible is facing forward, meeting the task head-on rather than half-yanking and half-dawdling."

WHAT IS A HABIT?

Notice that this chapter is called "Breaking *Old* Habits." It says nothing about *bad* habits. A habit is just something you have gotten so used to doing a certain way, that it is going to take some mighty charming work by every part of your mind to change. Honoring the way you do something now with the title "bad" only glamorizes the habit.

You are never the "victim" of your habits. Each habit is something that you have constructed carefully and deliberately over a period of time to simplify your daily decision-making process. Habits provide efficiency in the midst of confusing choices, safety in the midst of danger, and comfort in the face of distress. Habits are your personal rituals, as important if not as ingrained as society's rituals. Habits protect you. Don't give up a habit until you're sure you are better off without it.

Sometimes we simply outgrow a habit. We no longer need to suck our thumb or scuff our shoes on the fence or twist our pigtails. Every part of the mind agrees to give it up. At other times our mental executive determines that a habit no longer provides efficiency or protection. The habits that most commonly get in our way and become candidates for change are eating patterns, smoking, drinking, drug use, and nonproductive ways of managing time, money, personal possessions, and our health.

COMPULSIONS

When is a habit not a habit? Habitual behavior that is used to fill a "hole" in someone's life, to mask or block a more frightening behavior, is called a compulsion. Compulsions are also self-designed to be protective, but the subject loses control over them and feels powerless to stop, even when they produce irrational, dangerous or destructive behavior. Consider the fates of compulsive gamblers, kleptomaniacs, or anorexics. Compulsions are outside the help that any book can give. If you suspect that you have a compulsion, not a habit, and you want to change, you should seek professional help.

EXTREMES

Most of us can remember a strongly unpleasant experience in our childhood. One of the most interesting and quirky things we humans do is to recreate extremely negative childhood experiences in one of two absolutely opposite ways: We either do the same thing or we do the opposite. No in-between. We cope with these psychic bruises by recreating and imitating the past or by reviling and rejecting it totally.

The child of an alcoholic parent will likely be either an alcoholic or a teetotaler, but probably not a moderate social drinker.

Someone who lived in chaos as a child will tend to be either a slob or compulsively neat, but not someone who enjoys moderate order. The offspring of a workaholic will usually respond by being either a driven striver or an unconnected drifter, but rarely by enjoying a balance of work and recreation.

The two children of the champion skinflint, Hetty Green, illustrate this either/or phenomenon. Hetty was known in the 19th century as the world's richest woman. She was also a miser. She and her children lived like paupers. Her young son even lost his leg after a minor injury because she was too cheap to pay a doctor, dragging him from charity clinic to charity clinic until it was too late.

Arthur H. Lewis tells the whole fantastic story in his book *The Day They Shook the Plum Tree*. Hetty Green's millions were eventually inherited by her two children. Her daughter chose to live modestly, keeping her $31 million in an interest-free bank account. Her son became an expansive philanthropist and a bon vivant who spent $3 million a year with equal enthusiasm on yachts, stamps, politics, diamond-studded chastity belts, pornography, orchid culture, and young wards. When he died, the assessors spent many days inventorying his possessions which also included coins, bins of loose jewelry ($20 million in jewels lying about just one of his four homes), 149 pounds of jigsaw puzzles (bought all at once from Milton H. Bradley), a jewel-encrusted chamber pot (used), and an unusual object, mounted and hung in an entrance hall, which ultimately was identified as the 14-foot stuffed penis of a whale.

Some folks delight in citing their parents as the source of all their foibles. Considering how contrary children can be to even reasonable requests, this is hard to accept. Fortunately most of us, despite the usual array of childhood traumas, fall easily into the so-called happy medium. But a child that has been damaged by extremes requires extra portions of mental health and resilience and strength as an adult to follow a comfortable middle path.

DEALING WITH CIGARETTES

Maggie had decided to give up smoking, but she kept having "just one more." As Winston Churchill said, "Giving up smoking is easy. I've done it dozens of times." Sir Winston and Maggie kept signing a contract with their mental executive, but one or more of the other parts of the mind sabotaged the boss. It was the little guys against the big guy, and the little guys won—a heartening finale for fairy tales but not for your health.

Maggie couldn't succeed until all parts of her mind signed the contract to quit smoking. Here's how she finally did it.

meeting of the minds

Executive Part: "Stop smoking!"

Organizing Part: (*with infuriating logic*) "Smoking causes cancer. You'll have fewer colds and respiratory infections, greater self-respect, new confidence for other tasks, more stamina, less expense, clean air and a cleaner home free from cigarette burns and ashes, fresher breath, and more sex appeal. You'd be stupid to keep smoking!"

Knowing Part: "But *you* don't have to go through the agony I do. It feels like fingernails are clawing at the inside of my lungs! Just one puff and I'll feel human again."

Reacting Part: "I'm torn. I'd like all those nice things you describe, but I need a fix right *now*. How can I invest emotional energy in the future when the present is so miserable? My image of myself now is of a weak, ineffective human being. I'm beat. I'm hooked."

Organizing Part: "Your aunt died of lung cancer and she was just a few years older than you are now."

Knowing Part: "I refuse to relate that information to myself. I'm different."

Reacting Part: "But it makes me scared! Quick, calm me down with something soothing. What do you do when you want to be soothed?"

Knowing Part: (*helpfully*) "I have this lovely, soothing ritual of pulling out a cigarette, rolling it in my fingers, lighting it, inhaling, watching the smoke. . . ."

Organizing Part: "There you go, failing again. I tell you and tell you, but you never listen to me. You'll be the death of me yet!"

Wondering Part: "Hey, wait, you guys. I want to tell you a story that will make you forget all that. Listen!" (*Begins to create a fantasy—ideally while in a relaxed state, for example, at bedtime, but anywhere will work*) "I'm in an enchanted, peaceful place. There's a sparkling white field of unbroken snow near an icy stream. I'm wrapped up in something warm and cozy, but the cool air feels soothing on my cheeks. All the tension is draining out of me." (*The mind responds with signals to relax the muscles.*) "Now I'm walking through the spotless white snow. My feet are scuffing the sparkling powder and I can feel the soft crunch under my boots."

Knowing Part: "But I hurt!"

Wondering Part: "Listen! I stop and take a deep breath. My lungs take in bright, clean air. It's an amazing smell and I focus on it to savor every nuance. I taste the delicate tang of snowflakes on my tongue." (*The mind is distracted by a sharp twinge of discomfort.*) "Hey, pay attention! There's a slight tickle in my lungs, so I concentrate on how good my warm coat feels against the tingle of the cold air. I feel great! I can do just about anything—look at how I've created this special place! And I can do it any time I want to."

Reacting Part: "That was beautiful. I feel more comfortable. And smart, too."

Organizing Part: "I'll remind you to tell me another story whenever I need one. I'm very good at reminding."

Knowing Part: "Could we try a tropical rain forest the next time? What do you suppose frangipani smells like? Oh, oh, here comes another twinge. I'm going to interpret it as ice-cold mountain air. Brrrr."

Maggie replaced her *goal* of never smoking again with a *mission* to create healthy lungs. That way, a slip or two along the way wasn't proof of her worthlessness and inability to control her own life and body. Each cigarette-free day of improved health was proof that her mission was on track, despite the rarer and rarer setbacks.

Maggie also gave herself some cues that would trigger her new behavior by addressing the needs of each of her minds. She decided to use the craving sensation of her lungs to initiate a fantasy interpretation of breathing some new, exciting air. She created a host of fantasies that took her around the world and to other planets. If the physical discomfort was really strong, she could choose fantasies of *power* that incorporated this sensation: overseeing caldrons of molten metal in a steel mill, successfully crossing a sulfurous chasm on Venus. The tension that used to make Maggie reach for a cigarette now was a signal to fantasize while doing a set of muscle exercises, tensing and relaxing the different parts of her body in a playful sequence. She could do this anywhere, during a conference or at a bus stop.

To "have something to do with my hands," Maggie invested in professional manicures and tried different colors of nail polish. Then she practiced posing her hands in graceful attitudes, concentrating on choosing the best ones and noticing how the yellow stains were fading from her fingers.

Most people who smoke use the pause for inhaling to marshal their thoughts during a conversation. Tapping the cigarette on an ashtray lets them avoid the eyes of their companions momentarily. Maggie decided that she would be very uncomfortable without these ritual thought-collecting procedures. Some options she considered were getting a small lap dog (rejected as inappropriate for use at the office) and wearing a charm bracelet that would need to be untangled periodically. Glasses that must be taken on and off and located in pockets are also good space-makers in conversation.

Besides being physically addictive, smoking involves many personal rituals. These need to be replaced with new ones that provide similar supports. Since Maggie usually had a cigarette when the morning coffee wagon came around the office, she decided to use this arrival to cue a flood of tranquility and self-esteem. This took practice, but eventually she became so successful that she bought a tiny silver wagon for her new charm bracelet. This talisman became her symbol of her ability to get through stressful situations.

DEALING WITH FOOD

Society gives us a very mixed message about eating. Open any magazine for women and you'll find more than 50 color photos of succulent dishes plus the latest foolproof diet. Open a magazine for men and you'll find scowling, flat-stomached athletes plus ads for beer, whiskey, and restaurants that specialize in high-calorie "power lunches."

Women are especially vulnerable to distorted body images. The body idealized by fashion magazines is actually a freak. It has no more to do with a healthy female human than did wasp-waists, Ubangi lips, or Chinese bound feet. However, culture is so powerful that many women develop eating disorders and profound self-loathing trying to mimic this distorted model of beauty. Anorexia and bulimia are recognized illnesses requiring medical and psychological treatment. Men don't fare much better, presented with role models of men in their sixties and seventies who maintain the body of a well-muscled teenager.

While thousands of people worldwide starve to death every day, losing weight is a nationwide obsession in America. Putting aside this profoundly disturbing moral paradox, most of us could benefit from improving our diet. This means eating food that is adequate in nutrition and calories while it provides a feast for the eyes, delights the taste buds, and acts as a spiritual link with the nurturing and nourishing of our past. This can be a tall order when our fondly remembered childhood foods consisted chiefly of hot dogs and cupcakes. Nevertheless, an inventive mind can be stimulated to reframe childhood food experiences to provide supportive eating models for adults.

One reason that reducing diets fail so miserably is that they ignore most of the ways that food is processed by the parts of the *mind.* Preparing and eating food is an essential ritual in every society, yet these comforting rituals—sharing, discussing, comparing, savoring, celebrating, nurturing, recalling past pleasures—are forbidden the dieter. Traditional diet foods are usually eaten alone, often during a time when the diner is struggling with feelings of self-dislike. If company is around, the dieter is likely to be self-conscious and embarrassed, perhaps even teased or tempted by others in the group. "Diet" foods seldom trigger rich, nostalgic images of nurturing, comfort, delight.

People rarely rate themselves as a success or failure at nourishing themselves, but they sure know when they have "failed" at losing weight. Those who lose weight for a long time and then regain some of it don't see themselves as succeeding. They have failed utterly, terribly, and forever. They have no guilt about not getting enough essential nutrients, but getting too many calories is a capital offense. When this happens occasionally, it can produce what is called the "what the hell" effect.

There *is* a secret to lifelong weight maintenance, but it is rarely found in diet books or "goal" books. Are you ready? Here it is: Don't frame your intended weight loss as a goal, to be reached and then maintained with struggle, or else lost. Instead, reframe your ideal body image as a *process*: "My mission is to care for my body in every way and I possess the ability to do that. No one knows my body as well as I do. I am totally responsive to my many needs, and I'm smart enough to figure out how to fulfill them in the best way possible. This includes the most delicious food I can imagine, rich and varied, and totally fulfilling my nutritional and emotional needs."

Tell yourself, "I have many wonderful memories of magical times involving food. If I'm smart enough to recreate and relive these enriching moments, I'm also smart enough to invent new rituals with these foods, celebrating my lifetime mission of a healthy body."

Address the food needs of the different parts of your mind. Provide patterns and rituals for the organizing part. Set the wondering part to work creating and recreating these rituals in healthful new ways, so the sight and taste of nourishing foods brings a flood of warm, supportive feelings. The knowing part of your mind loves colors, textures, flavors. Satisfy it. It also loves information about things. Turn it loose on facts about B vitamins, carbohydrates, fiber, and what quantities you need to nourish and invigorate you. We no longer believe that it's simply "calories in, calories out." Our bodies are much more sophisticated than that. The knowing part can enjoy discovering new things about nutrition, separating fact from fad and even fraud in the multimillion dollar Diet Business. The emotional part wants comfort, pleasure, and rewards. It fears change. Assure it that new joys and rewards are in store, especially the exciting sensations of a happy body.

If your comforting rituals of the past involve a huge spaghetti dinner with all the trimmings eaten with friends, then a lonely diet dinner of celery root "pasta" covered with pureed beets for "tomato sauce" just doesn't make it! When you eat spaghetti alone, part of you wants to recreate the warm feelings of companionship and abundance, comfort and happiness that the ritual recalls. Maybe you can establish new rituals with supportive, exciting people that involve equally supportive foods. But even if you can't go back and reexperience these pleasant rituals with the same people, you can reframe the memory. Select the food elements that fit your new body-support system. Remember the crisp salads, the succulent vegetables of the antipasto, the tinkling glasses of ice water, the delicate lemon gelato for dessert? Focus on those taste delights as you reexperience the warmth and pleasure of a fulfilling eating experience in a comforting setting.

Was your ritual meal pizza and beer? It is possible to make mouth-watering pizza with crispy crust, flavorful tomato sauce, and hot, runny low-fat cheese. Focus on the textures, the tastes of the broiled mushrooms and tangy green peppers. Stroke the cool, bubbling glass, now full of sparkling water, as you listen to the funniest jokes you've ever heard.

Was your special ritual a hot fudge banana split in a glistening pedestal dish at the ice cream parlor? Treat yourself to a cut glass dish and fill it with mounds of cottage cheese and fruits, sprinkled with nuts and topped with yogurt and a cherry. As you eat, re-experience the suppressed exhilaration of being in the white-walled ice cream parlor, dressed in your best after a special movie or theater matinee. Your head still spins with the pleasure and excitement of the show you've just seen. What a treat!

TAKING CHARGE OF MONEY

Handling your financial affairs can be fascinating or it may seem deadly dull. If you hate the nuts and bolts of finances, this may be a defensive block. In that list of emotion-charged words— "love," "sex," "money," "death"—money ranks pretty high for most people. Money comes with a lot of emotional baggage.

If money can't buy happiness, it can usually buy respect, comfort, power, and a fair degree of health. Like sex, it can be used as a weapon or a symbol of affection. Like love, it can produce self-esteem and a sense of security. Like death, it has the power to bring out the best and the worst in people. No, money is far from boring.

So why do so many people shun balancing their checkbooks and keeping track of their income and outgo? Even financial advisors to the President have been known to put off filing their income tax. Financial extremes represent compulsions. Spending far more than you make or depriving yourself of necessities when you can afford them are irrational behaviors and outside the scope of this book. But the *habit* of blocking out or distorting the financial details of your life can be changed.

Perhaps you "don't want to know" your bank balance for fear that it is less than you'd like. You enjoy the warm illusion of affluence which a reality based bottom line would squelch. Or, through habit, you've left those "boring financial details" to someone else, either in their role as a protector or as a servant. Such details are either beneath you or beyond you. Well, since you're smart enough to be reading this book, you are also smart enough to take a few minutes to understand interest, taxes, mortgages, investments, percentages, payment schedules and plain old addition and subtraction.

If the process of working with numbers puts up an instant block, charm the organizing and learning parts of your mind by flattering them about their previous successes in difficult areas. The so-called "fear of math" is a habit. If you are ready to change it, get your imagination to whisper seductive promises of glittering insights and newfound controls. It doesn't matter whether your annual income is $500,000 or $5,000. The replacement habit is far more exciting. We are talking *power!* Raw, brutal, thrilling, sensual power over part of your life.

If the product of your energies, the realistic picture of your finances, threatens your fantasy of being in control, ignoring the reality can become a habit too. It is a habit to say, "I can't afford it," or alternately "I deserve it," to every possibility without thinking. The habit saves the time and energy of making a realistic evaluation. Maybe you *can* afford it and actually need it. Maybe you *don't* deserve it, or at least you don't deserve the anguish and disruption of the resulting debt.

Stinginess and extravagance are two ways of *feeling* in control without *being* in control. Here a conspiracy of the organizing and wondering parts of the mind is needed to overcome emotional resistance. The playful wondering part starts a game of "What if . . . ?" "What if I thought about each expenditure instead of responding automatically? How would I feel? Would I be scared? Or happy?" The analytical organizing part jumps in with structures for data, sometimes appealing to the mental executive for wise words: "You can reward yourself in ways that don't hurt you" or "Your pleasure needn't be in inverse ratio to price." Understandably, your emotional reacting part will be uncomfortable while you discard old habits, so keep it busy experiencing the new excitement and pleasure of dealing realistically with this important part of your life.

TAKING CHARGE OF YOUR POSSESSIONS

Short of moving to a monastic cell with a straw pallet and a begging bowl, most of us must cope with too many possessions. Some are of our choosing. Some, mainly bits of paper, are forced on us by society. (Intriguingly, poor people, or those who were poor as children, often deal with many more possessions than those who are better off because they are more conscious of the possibilities for reusing broken and worn-out objects: "It might come in handy someday.")

Organizing possessions is one of the chief passions of the organizing part of your mind, something it does very well. People who say, "Oh, I'm just not a good organizer," ignore all the hard work their mind does for them, choosing between this and that every minute of every day. (One theory of dreams suggests that the mind goes on organizing while you sleep, taking all the useless and unattached bits floating about and fashioning them into vaguely plausible sequences so your minds can discard them. Dreams become wastebaskets for surplus information.)

Unfortunately the organizing part must deal with a lot of distractions and conflicting messages from the other parts of the mind. A messy room or desk can represent safety, privacy, a source of attention and nurturing from others, punishment, or a good excuse for lack of productivity. Accumulations of objects can represent security, love, comfort, power, protection. Things that we choose to surround us become extensions of ourselves, representing us both to others and to ourselves.

 **meeting of the minds**

Executive Part: "Store things for easy retrieval."
Wondering Part: (*Gets excited about storage props.*)
Organizing Part: "I know how!"
Reacting Part: "I won't because I prefer the familiar feeling of chaos, of getting attention if only from myself. If I harass myself the way my mother harassed me, I won't lose my connection with her. Maybe she will pay attention to me, even though she's not here anymore."
Knowing Part: "I can still reexperience her attention. I'll constantly present my problem to others and then shoot down their offered solutions. That'll fix Mom!"
Wondering Part: (*Gets excited about the drama and attention.*)
Reacting Part: "Everyone is focused on me! Wow! Even if it is embarrassing, it's thrilling. Like walking down the street naked, only more acceptable."

Asking someone to give up this source of energy is like asking a junkie to give up dope. Adrenaline is a powerful drug. No amount of pain can persuade the habitually disorganized to relinquish such a surefire fix. This is one case where "hitting bottom" probably won't motivate a change. The payoff at the bottom is even greater than on the way down. Any self-destructive behavior with such a potent payoff is beyond the help of a book.

Moderate, everyday disorganization can be dealt with by conscious efforts combined with playful techniques and seductive rewards: "I'll have a cup of coffee after I file these letters." "Another set of shelves would let me alphabetize my books." "Honey, every time you put a toy away on the shelf, I'll make a silly face for you." Assess the situation (knowing part), evaluate any conflicts (reacting part), come up with structures (organizing part), and provide energy for the task (wondering part). Overcome habits like tossing your dirty socks on the coffee table by making up games: "I'll give myself ten points for getting my socks into the hamper before Mildred brings in the martinis."

Losing keys, glasses, or important papers in moments of distraction doesn't come under the heading of "habit" unless you usually lose these things. If the phone rings just as you come in the door, try the "photo" technique for your keys. Set them down anywhere and raise your hands, pantomiming taking a photo of them. Say, "I am putting my keys on the kitchen counter," as you click the imaginary camera. Then answer the phone. It takes less than ten seconds. Afterwards you have three ways to remember where the keys are: verbal, visual, and kinesthetic.

Some people collect masses of things, eager to "have" them, but then lose them in the jumble. One man videotapes many hours each week and has 4,000 videotapes, stacked in cardboard cartons that totally fill one room. He brags about "having" this or that event on tape, but cannot locate the proper tape to show to potential viewers. The tape he wants is rarely in the box he thinks it's in. But his mental executive rejects the truism: *If you can't find it, you don't have it.* When people are comfortable thinking that "it's here somewhere" and they manage to find clean clothes, food, and unpaid bills, then their mess is chiefly of concern to their cohabitants and the local health department. But when finding things becomes a *personal* concern, then they are ready to try a different habit.

If you live with such a person, try making organization a delightful game with lots of ridiculous rules: "Bank statements in the bread box, bills under the bird cage. Bread equals money, bird equals bill. Get it?" Once putting something in the same place each time becomes a habit, the place can be changed. The mind that fails to grasp putting clean laundry in a drawer is amazingly adept at finding socks and underwear temporarily filed alphabetically in a filing cabinet. Books stacked all over the tables and floor can find homes in the pantry, novels with the noodles, biographies with baking supplies, etc. Very soon the extra energy used to file and retrieve these objects can be diverted to storing them in more conventional settings.

Some people motivate major cleanups by inviting guests for a time some days or weeks away. Enthusiastic collectors who can't stop acquiring long enough to organize their acquisitions can sometimes be moved to do so by agreeing to a public presentation of their treasures to a visiting expert or a local club on a specific future date.

If *you* are the one who drops things, you know better than anyone else what will entice and lure you into the comfortable, powerful position of being in control, of actually *possessing* the objects around you instead of being possessed *by* them. Sometimes fear of outside intrusion is a real issue. It's like breaking your toys so your brother won't try to borrow them, or asking for the turkey gizzard at a banquet because no one is likely to challenge you for it: "It's not much but it's all mine." Ask yourself if this protection is really still necessary. If not, strike a bargain with your emotional self: "I'm going to organize my possessions; there's going to be a really nice payoff for you in this new process, so you let me know any time you feel uncomfortable and we'll work it out."

TAKING CHARGE OF YOUR HEALTH

At 20, we all know that we are immortal. At 40, we all suspect otherwise. Somewhere in between, if we are lucky, we discard the habits acquired in our immortal youth and choose new ones to make the most of the incredible physical mechanism that carries our minds around.

By now you've noted that executive directives from the mind like "Exercise more" or "Floss after every meal" don't always work. What are your health goals? Jot them down. Some typical ones are:

- Exercise more efficiently and consistently.

- Eat more healthful foods.

- Rest/relax more.

- Control stress and tension.

- Really take care of my teeth.

- Drink/smoke/take pills less.

- Keep my hair, skin, fingernails really healthy.

Orders from our mental executive are like New Year's resolutions. They are "oughts" (musts) that quickly turn into "oughts" (zeros) because they have no support from the other parts of the mind. People who are dedicated to nurturing and pampering themselves with healthful routines are rarely lured from this pleasure by outside distractions. Every part of their minds has agreed to support certain routines and to overcome problems that try to intervene.

Part of finding the time for health routines involves reframing priorities. Caring for yourself is not selfish. Being selfless does not mean having no self. You give your best to others when you have something to give. No matter how demanding your schedule, you *must* make time for maintaining your own equipment. The "time" that most people complain about losing is not the actual minutes of the activities but the time spent trying to justify skipping them just this once. A clever organizer can piggyback health routines onto other regular activities with little loss in actual time. Floss your teeth while watching the television news. Dry your hair while reading the newspaper. Pick simple exercises to do while shopping, doing housework, on the phone, waiting in line at the bank. Get friends to go along for chatty walks. Stretch out and nap at lunchtime. Stop for a quick swim every night on your way home from work. Don't wait until you "have" time. Make time. A minute here, two minutes there will do it. In no other area of our life are habits so essential.

IMPULSE CONTROL

At first glance, compulsive and impulsive behavior would seem to be opposites, but they are actually two sides of the same coin. Most of us can vow to change our behavior, to give up certain habits, and then a seemingly irresistible impulse destroys our self-esteem and we conclude that we are just too weak, we'd better give in.

Impulses represent the rebellion of one part of the mind against the activities agreed to by the others. Most often the rebel is the reacting or wondering part, but it can also be the knowing part, desperate for stimulation, or the organizing part, eager for structure. Occasionally it is even the mental executive that makes an altruistic, unilateral, spur-of-the-moment decision—that is, a totally illogical, self-sacrificing gesture such as rushing into a burning building to save a child.

We rarely want to control these noble impulses, but there are some less helpful ones that we could do without. Impulse control starts with recognizing that one mind is not getting what it wants and trying to negotiate with it, before doing the impulsive thing. Here are some conversations of an impulsive shopper:

Manual of Procedures: Your possessions represent your intelligence and taste to the world. (*If it's on sale, buy it!*)

meeting of the minds

Knowing Part: "I need clothes, books, beautiful surroundings, the latest in electronic equipment and gadgets. I have strong aesthetic needs, love the stimulation of all the senses with colors and textures, the intellectual pleasures of discovering the newest things, the excitement of interacting with clerks and showing them how knowledgeable I am, the thrill of possessing the fastest, sleekest car, of being seen by others as smart, strong, attractive, powerful."

Organizing Part: "You can't afford it." (*Note the "you"!*)

Reacting Part: "I love the fun, heightened awareness, intensity, sense of power when shopping."

Wondering Part: "What's new? What are people wearing, using, reading, listening to? How does that work? How will it make my life better? How will others react to me if I have it?"

Reacting Part: "I deserve this."

Executive Part: "Let's have a meeting so each mind can get something of what it wants."

HABITS: LOVE THEM OR CHANGE THEM

Teaching yourself to do something so consistently that no one else can influence you to stop it—acquiring a habit—is quite an accomplishment. It took a lot of strength to create that habit. That habit represents a lot of your personal power. Use that same power to learn to go somewhere else. Use it like jujitsu to leverage yourself to where you want to be. "Brains don't learn to get results," says psychologist Richard Bandler, "they learn to go in directions." Plan! Without planning, you easily can go where you don't want or intend to go. Habits are like railroad tracks. You lay them down with a lot of effort so that later you can get where you want to be, smoothly and easily.

REWARD OR PUNISHMENT

The basis of all self-disciplined behavior is the ability to wait for a desired result—that is, to delay gratification. Delayed gratification means you consciously predict the future result of an immediate action, and then you evaluate whether a pleasure right now will delay or destroy a larger future pleasure.

Delayed rewards are tricky. The fact that a reward is delayed doesn't guarantee that its value will increase. Clinical studies have shown that gratification, like justice, can be delayed so long that it becomes worthless; the test subjects no longer desire the reward. An example in the real world could be the benefits of delaying marriage until financial independence is established. Most people would feel that any advantages of this delay decrease sharply after the age of 30 and stop altogether after 60.

Researchers have studied the effectiveness of both self-reward and self-punishment in controlling impulsive behavior. Consistently these studies have shown that self-punishment is almost totally ineffective in modifying habits. In one study at Penn State University, published in the *Journal of Consulting and Clinical Psychology*, a group of dieters who were taught to follow a system of self-punishment did not lose significantly more weight than a control group that was not trying to lose weight. Berating yourself doesn't work and can even make it harder to get change.

Reward systems show far better results. A system of self-reward combined with self-monitoring and strong sensory goals has consistently proven the most effective strategy for altering even the most ingrained habits.

There are three criteria for an appropriate self-reward:

1. It should be accessible and controllable.

2. It should have a high reward value to you.

3. You would like to experience this reward more often than you are currently experiencing it.

Some rewards you might consider are: watching a favorite TV program, listening to music, reading for pleasure, doing a crossword puzzle, window-shopping, browsing in a favorite store, relaxing in a special place, jogging, taking a stroll, sports, playing a game, phoning a friend, taking a luxurious bath, getting a massage, drinking special beverages and eating special foods, wearing clothes you rarely wear (dressing up or down), sitting quietly doing absolutely nothing. Customize your own list.

Reward contracts work very well for some people, even when they feel a little silly about such a childish device. In fact, the playful nature of such a deal can make "winning" as intensely serious as a pro football game.

Here's a contract form:

Reward Contract

I will complete the following task that I have selected as a step toward reaching my goal: _____

in the following time frame: _____

My success will be measurable by: _____

This goal is supported by my mission which is: _____

_____

My reward will be: _____

(clearly state number, duration, etc.)

Note the place for writing your goal. This goal must be specific, not general, and must have a time frame. For example:

Not	But
Quit smoking.	Don't smoke for the next five minutes/two hours/day.
Be thin.	Lose two pounds a week for six weeks.
Be neat.	Put all my clothes in the hamper for the next three days.
Control my money.	Balance my checking account within 24 hours after receiving my next two bank statements.
Get ahead at work.	For the next three days, greet everyone I meet in the morning by name with a friendly smile: "Good morning, Tom." "Good morning, Mr. Harcourt."

At the end of the contract term, you negotiate an extension until the new behavior becomes habit. Then write a new contract.

Human beings are contradictory creatures. We crave the new, the different, will gladly discard a perfectly good gadget, idea, or spouse for a newer model, yet we can be totally resistant to change. Even if what we're doing doesn't work, we'll do it again and again, harder, faster, longer, louder. Go figure.

Making a game out of change has sound scientific support. A technical definition of self control, based on the work of the Russian neuropsychologist Aleksandr R. Luria, and of prominent cognitive-behavioral American psychologists is offered by Marquette University's Marvin Berkowitz, Ph.D., in his book *Peer Conflict and Psychological Growth,* "Self control is the ability to intentionally manipulate covert mental events, most notably inner speech and images, in order to regulate one's own behavior." That "inner speech" refers to the conversations that go on constantly among our minds. The "covert mental events" could be called cues—the signals we give ourselves when it is time to do something. We'll discuss more ways to create and use these cues in chapter 13.

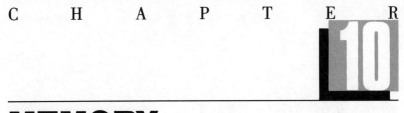

MEMORY

Except for torturing rats, probably more psychologists'
time has gone into studying memory than any
other subject.

—Richard Bandler,
Using Your Brain—For a Change

Every part of your mind participates in remembering. Memory is an activity, not a place. The process records selected information provided by all the parts. The more parts that contribute to writing a specific memory, the more ways you have to retrieve it later from the as-yet-undiscovered secret codes of the neural transmitters in your brain. Remembering a particular thing with several different parts of your mind is like putting a collar *and* a harness *and* a leash on a greased pig. You have more chances of grabbing it when you want it.

WHAT THE MIND REMEMBERS

Let's look at our impressions of meeting someone new, as seen by the different parts of your mind.

meeting of the minds

Knowing Part: "Firm handshake, blue shirt, cologne, taller than I am."

Wondering Part: "Looks like he has a sense of humor. Is that a toupee? I wonder where he bought his suit."

Organizing Part: "His company is our biggest client. He's only an assistant vice president. How does he pronounce his last name?"

Reacting Part: "He might not like me. Do I like him?"

Silent Part: (*slight adrenaline rush, sweaty palms*)

Executive Part: "Well, Frank, I've been looking forward to meeting you!"

If sufficiently stimulated, our memory will file some of these conversations. Of course, any part of our mind can sabotage the others. The most frequent culprit is the reacting part which responds with a tangle of overriding messages: "Is my fly open? Is that ketchup on my tie? What does he think of me? Oops, I just spilled his drink down his front." These urgent personal messages will probably be recorded while the others are discarded.

MISLABELING TO REMEMBER

Psychologists Ornstein and Sobel say in their writings, ". . . our illusion of a stable outside world is a *consistent illusion that the brain creates*." In other words, we deliberately distort reality so it makes sense. Otherwise we couldn't sort and store decades of information and then retrieve everything under a particular title at one time.

This distortion is both bad and good, writes Anthony Greenwald in *American Psychologist*. It's bad because we are misremembering, often dangerously simplifying or deliberately mislabeling something.

It's good because we use our energy to store information instead of constantly revising and re-indexing our card catalogue. Ideally we will be conscious of our mislabeling and reevaluate the information when we retrieve it: Picasso is a "French" painter, but he was born in Spain.

USING ALL OF THE MIND

Remembering what we want to remember and forgetting what we want to forget are constant processes of our busy multiple-part mind. Let's look at how each part can help the remembering operation.

meeting of the minds

Knowing Part: "How does it feel to the touch—rough, smooth, pleasant, unpleasant, painful? What does it look like? Sound like? Smell like? Taste like? Remind me of?" (*Wallow in all the sensations.*)

Wondering Part: "What fun! Look at that! What if it . . . ? What if I . . . ? Could it also be . . . ? Isn't it something like . . . ?"

Organizing Part: "How important is it? How does it relate to other things, other experiences? Is it better or worse, bigger or smaller? How does it fit into the already established sequence of things? Does that sequence change because of it?"

Reacting Part: "Do I respond with happiness or anger? Sorrow? Boredom? Jealousy? Anxiety?" (*Pass this information on to your mental executive for analysis and feedback.*)

Executive Part: "I decide to remember this."

Your mental executive could just as easily decide to discard the information. Or it could want to remember—"This is important, this is valuable"—but the other parts of the mind might be too distracted or worn out to pay attention.

REMEMBERING NAMES

Let's imagine that you have arrived at a party. Your approaching host is about to introduce you to another guest. How can all your minds become involved?

meeting of the minds

Executive Part: (*Update Your* Manual of Procedures *on names*) If you try to see a person and hear her name at the same time, you will get overlapping images that will decay faster. *See before you hear.*

Reacting Part: Be impressed *before* you hear a name you want to remember. How do you *feel* as you concentrate on a new person? Positively? Negatively? Or is the person neutral?

Knowing Part: Refuse to hear the name of a new person until you have registered her height, weight, color of hair, skin, and eyes. Notice clothing colors, shapes, line, textures, style, and degree of ordinariness—what it means to you when a person dresses this way.

Organizing Part: Is she like anyone else you've met before? How? Every person you meet is interpreted in some way by your past experience with similar characters. Concentrate on these connections so you'll have memorable associations.

Wondering Part: If the person you want to remember is not outstanding, if he seems to blend into the background, you might envision him in the role of Invisible Person. Give him an imaginary context. Pretend he is incognito, an undercover agent or celebrity. Supply the missing drama to capture your attention when a low-profile person isn't putting out energy toward your noticing him. Notice the information supplied by your Knowing Mind and ask what role is currently being announced through the nonverbal language of clothing, makeup, hair style.

Knowing Part: Now that you have impressed yourself with visual and emotional stimuli, *listen* to the name. Ask yourself, "Does this person's name match my impression of its owner?" Whether the answer is yes or no, you will be locking in new information. You will have paid attention to differences as well as similarities.

Organizing Part: Ask yourself if the name means something in English—Jack, Tree, Houseman. Does it mean something in another language? Bijou, Schwartz, Verdi? Or of non-English origin but having an English meaning? Sing, Singh, Synge?

Is it the same name as that of: Someone you know? A celebrity? A literary or historical figure? A profession or occupation? A geographic place? A bird—robin, jay; a jewel—ruby, opal, pearl; a flower—rose, iris; a month—April, May, June; a car—Dodge, Ford, Lincoln?

Are the first and last names both usually used as first names —Tony Bill? Or last names—Taylor Caldwell?

Does the last name contain "son"? If so, can you use the other name to imagine the person is shrinking into a smaller version, a "son" of the big thing?

Does the name rhyme with something familiar?

See how your Organizing Mind can help you find a familiar category to register visual and verbal impressions of someone new.

Wondering and Reacting Parts: Now make playful or naughty or peculiar associations that will lock together the name and face and all you want to know about the person for permanent storage and easy retrieval.

Knowing Part: Finally enjoy the sounds of new names. They can be interpreted as music. As you hear them, repeat them. You won't be floored if you are introduced to Mike Csikszentmihalyi because you know it sounds like "6 cents me holly." Just mimic the sounds and enjoy surprising the people whose names used to be hard to pronounce.

YOUR MEMORY CAPACITY

A typical adult brain contains between 15 and 100 trillion neurons, depending on who's counting. If we accept the lower figure, this means that you can remember two-to-the-ten-billionth-power bits of information. Just to write out this number that represents the items your mind is capable of holding, you would have to write a zero a second for 90 years, according to neurologist Richard M. Restak in his book *The Brain: The Last Frontier.* Popular science writer Carl Sagan uses the higher figure in *Cosmos,* representing the equivalent of the information in 20 million encyclopedia volumes.

How much you actually do remember is determined by:

- Your inborn capacity to remember (obviously much higher than you sometimes think!).

- Your training for efficient collection, intelligent interpretation, and maximum storage of information (sometimes called "education").

- Your enthusiasm for remembering a particular thing.

- The effect of things you learned before ("proactive interference") and things you learned after ("retroactive interference") on the particular thing you want to remember.

- The effect of physical, mechanical, and emotional blocks.

Physical blocks can be caused by fatigue, tension, illness, poor nutrition, some prescription and recreational drugs, alcohol, nicotine, and lack of exercise.

A mechanical block means you didn't record the information in the first place. Common mechanical blocks include distractions, either when you encountered the information or when you try to recall it, and misinterpreting the information so that it is either discarded or filed in the wrong place. For instance, a casual stroller probably wouldn't even notice some odd-looking rocks along a path. The same pebbles might send a geologist or paleontologist into transports of ecstasy and provide the basis for a lifetime of study.

Emotional blocks are usually protective in nature. Sometimes we hang onto these protective blocks long after we have outgrown their usefulness. Forgetting becomes a habit. Much of my work with "blocked" people is watching them realize that they no longer need this particular form of protection. Therapists love discovering these emotional memory blocks because they are usually fascinating, dramatic, and relatively easy to overcome.

Memory blocks don't necessarily mean that someone doesn't care. Sometimes we block things because we care a lot. Our Reacting

Mind sends out such strong distress signals at the thought of loss or change that the Knowing Mind shuts down and stops noticing.

SELECTIVE FORGETTING

Some things are better forgotten. You've probably heard that phrase and maybe balked at it because it referred to overlooking injustice or corruption, or ignoring a blatant but embarrassing truth. However, there really are some things that we should learn to forget.

Do you want to reexperience every pain and sorrow vividly? Recall every slight or unpleasantness? Every error or failure? We can remember the *lessons* of sad and difficult experiences without remembering the pain. We can learn to replace negative memories just as we replace faded flowers in a centerpiece. We move other, fresher blooms to a more prominent position or we bring in new flowers to fill the holes.

Selective forgetting is healthful. It's one of the big advantages that people have over computers. Instead of berating yourself over every memory lapse, learn to spot the ones that actually help you. A healthy person doesn't need to eradicate unpleasant or tragic memories, but will choose more valuable ones in their place, rehearsing these other mental images until they automatically replace the negative ones.

USING STRUCTURES

All the parts of our mind share two somewhat contradictory characteristics, say psychology experts Ornstein and Sobel:

1. They want to be stimulated.

2. They want to simplify incoming information.

Your inborn organizer loves having lots of bits to work with, but sometimes it can bog down and feel overwhelmed. Fortunately many natural and man-made structures exist for it to use. Male/female, child/adult, animal/plant are some examples of natural structures that can be recognized and experienced without the necessity of language. Language and numbers are artificial, man-made structures. Information is simplified by clustering it in groups, dividing it, stringing it in sequences, and choosing or rejecting parts so that the remainder forms a recognizable or acceptable pattern.

We remember things verbally by giving them labels. Phone numbers, addresses, lists of presidents and countries fall into this category. We remember things visually by their color and proportions. Recognizing faces, the paintings of Renoir, or the color vermilion uses visual memory, usually reinforced by putting verbal labels on the object. (There is some fascinating research on the ability to recognize color differences when no names exist for them.) Remembering how to type, drive a car, dance, or where the furniture is in your home are examples of kinesthetic memories—the whole-body recall of your body and the space around it. Most information is recalled in some combination of verbal, visual, and kinesthetic memory.

THE PEG SYSTEM

A playful way to recall sequences of things is called *mnemonics* or, more popularly, the "peg system." This technique dates back to Grecian times and got its name from the Greek goddess of memory, Mnemosyne. Simply put, you use a structure that you are already familiar with—the alphabet, numbers, the parts of your body, the rooms in your house—and mentally attach unfamiliar things to each familiar part. Then when you recall the sequence you know, the other items come along too.

You may want to remember your new material in a particular sequence or perhaps it doesn't matter. Either way, "pegging" it to something you already know makes it easier to recall. My book *Total Recall* describes a number of different memory systems. Some people find them very useful for everyday remembering; others choose another memory system called pencil and paper. The advantage of the peg system over making lists on paper is that you can do it any time, any place, in the dark, in the shower, driving down the highway. You might want to try the peg system just for fun.

In my memory seminars, I show people "How to Remember 20 Things in Less than Two Minutes." This is fairly spectacular, but it's actually incredibly easy to do. It's done with a peg system. People call out any 20 things at random and then I say them back in order. You can easily do the same thing and impress your friends at parties.

To remember 20 or 30 or even 1,000 things, it is essential to divide them into smaller units of 5 or 10. To prove this to yourself, notice that right now you can easily remember a million things in exact sequence: how to count from 1 to 1,000,000! Numbers can be used in the peg system, but most people do better with visual images.

Here is how to remember 20 things in less than two minutes, previously described in *Total Recall.* Start with your body. Bodies are especially good, always available for remembering shopping lists, the points of a speech, the sequence of streets, cities or railroad stations on a journey.

1. The top of your head: The first thing is clinging to the top of your head, an enormous, exotic hat. Will it fall off? Or the object you want to remember is stuck in your hair, oozing down over your face.

2. Your forehead: It's a billboard or flashing neon sign advertising the second object.

3. Your nose: It's a vending machine spurting out dozens of the third thing. Or the thing is growing out of your nose.

4. Your mouth: It's a tunnel with the fourth item driving in or pouring out. Or your teeth or tongue become the object.

5. Your throat: A transparent crystal cylinder that reminds you of Tiffany's window. The object it holds is very, very precious.

6. Your chest: Here the object is stored in duplicate like a pair of lungs.

7. Your belly button: The object is glued there or flashing there.

8. Your hips: A belly dancer's hip belt is strung with dozens of the eighth object. They move, clank, twinkle as you dance.

9. Your knees: You are kneeling on the ninth object. Is it pleasant? Comfortable? Awful?

10. Your feet: You stand on the tenth object. What does it feel like? What are your feet doing to the object?

For the next ten objects, you might choose one or two rooms in your house, or use the garage, or the backyard. Starting at the door, make a clockwise circuit of stationary objects, attaching the new information to them. Kitchens are great for this. They have stoves to burn things with, sinks to flood them, refrigerators to freeze them, toasters to pop them up, blenders to mince them, garbage disposals to chew them, and cabinets to shelve them. Bathrooms have tubs to soak things, toilets to flush them, sinks with faucets to spurt them, toilet paper dispensers to unreel them, showers to spray them, towel racks to drape them over. Living rooms have couches to smear or sink them into, lamps to light up, televisions to feature them or drip them over, bookcases to stuff them into, stereos to blast them or play tunes about them, fireplaces to burn them, telephones shaped like them. Here's how a bedroom might be used:

11. Bed: The object is snuggled in the covers, oozing over the sheets, flaunting itself, yawning, snoring.

12. Dresser: The object is dangling from the drawers, or it has been cut up to form the drawer pulls or it is glued all over the outside. The drawers can be used to store several pieces of information about the same thing.

13. Closet: The object is dangling from each hanger. Your clothes are soaked in it. It leaps out of shoe bags and hat boxes. It is a monster, waiting to leap out at you.

14. Chair: The legs are each your object. Or your object is sitting in the chair, smiling at you. Or the object itself is a chair on which you must sit.

15. Night table: Your object is a giant hollow lamp, flashing on and off. Or it is sitting in a glass of water, like false teeth. Or it has a clock face in it and it is ticking loudly.

Then on to another place. How about your backyard?

16. Flower bed: The object is growing. Dozens of little versions are smiling up at you from the leafy bed. Or it is huge, stomping your precious flowers. Stop!

17. Tree: Each leaf is a miniature object. Or your object is sitting in the branches as your dog snaps at its heels. Or it has replaced the tree, its bottom rooted in the ground.

18. Barbecue: You are cooking this object, rotating it slowly over the coals. Or it is putting out the fire, making you very annoyed.

19. Garage: Your object is blocking the door to the garage. It is so large you can barely get by. What will happen if you drive your car through it? Or it is nailed all over the sides of the garage like tiny shingles.

20. Tool shed: Be careful when you open the door—it is going to tumble out with all the rakes and brooms. It is tangled in the handles. Or it pours out when you open the door. Or it has flattened itself into a giant leaf rake.

Here's an alphabet version. Usually, using objects that start with the letter A like apple or ant can be confusing. (Do you want to buy apples or ant poison?) But you can construct a careful alphabet around something you are unlikely to be matching. Use animals for shopping lists. Fictional characters for phone calls you want to make. (Remember that "object" in these descriptions can also mean an action represented by an object. For instance, making a transaction at the bank can be represented by a deposit slip. Canceling tickets by phone would be represented by the ticket itself.)

An Alphabetical Animal Sequence:

1. Anteater: The little creature is busy snuffling up miniature versions of your object through his long nose. Or maybe the object is so oddly shaped, that the

anteater is staring at it in surprise, unsure how to eat it. Or a decorative statuette of an anteater has been carved or molded from your object. Ants eye the statue hungrily.

2. Bear: He is fishing in a stream for tasty salmon. Imagine his surprise when your object comes leaping upstream. Or your object is stuck in his fur and he frantically tries to remove it. Or he is chasing it up a tree.

3. Camel: Your object is packed in duplicate on the camel's two humps, flopping across the desert on the camel's back. Or it forms a canopy over the camel's rider. Or it dangles from the camel's blanket, trailing along behind in the hot sand.

4. Donkey: The donkey is kicking your object. It is flying through the air. The donkey's hooves are stomping it, marking their distinctive prints on it.

5. Elephant: Your object is gushing from the elephant's trunk. Or the beast is tossing your object up onto its back. Or it is stomping your object with its giant feet. Imagine round footprints on your object.

6. Fox: The fox's bushy tail is dragging through your object. Its little paws are each resting on your object. Your object is hanging out of the fox's sharp teeth as its bright eyes glitter.

7. Giraffe: Your object is sliding down the animal's long, graceful neck. Or the giraffe is wearing a hundred necklaces made up of your object. Hear them jangle or clatter or bump against each other.

8. Hamster: The hamster is running happily in its wheel, sending your object flying all over its cage. It burrows in it, chews it, swims in it.

9. Ibis: This bird that appears mainly in alphabet books and crossword puzzles is about to do the world another good turn. It is standing elegantly in a pool of your

object. Or its wings are made up of your object. Can it fly?

10. Jackal: Fierce and mean-looking, the jackal crouches over your object, tearing at it with its teeth and claws. Your object is very precious and the jackal guards it sullenly. Or the beast is suddenly inundated with your object. Will it enjoy the experience? Be angry? Be in pain? What will it do to wash the stuff off?

An Alphabetical Fictional Character Sequence:

1. Ahab: Ahab pursues the great white whale by throwing your object at Moby Dick. What is the whale's reaction? Imagine your object in the giant beast's mouth, sea water gushing over it as the whale's tiny eye glints. Or Ahab is rowing through a sea of this stuff.

2. Batman: The Caped Crusader is battling his way out of a giant tub of your object. Or he is rescuing your object from a villain. Or his Batmobile is about to drive through your object. Look out, Robin!

3. Cat in the Hat: Dr. Seuss's wily feline doffs his striped top hat and out tumbles your object. Or he devises one of his clever games with the item, getting you in trouble.

4. Dagwood: Dagwood is about to bite into a giant sandwich made with your object. Or, unawares, he is about to step on the thing at the top of the stairs. Or Daisy and her puppies are stuck in your object, coated with it, reeking of it, as Blondie stands amazed.

5. Elliot Ness: The G-man has his gun trained on your object, but he may be outwitted this time. Your object takes on a menacing form—it is huge, it is shaped like a gun, or dozens of it are in a cargo net over his head, waiting to tumble on him. Or he is tied up in a dungeon as your stuff pours in on him. Make this a real cliff-hanger.

6. Frankenstein: The good doctor's monster is stalking the streets, crying for this object. He heads straight for where he can get it. Imagine the look on the faces of the people there as he crashes through the wall, arms outstretched, shouting one word: ". . ."

7. Goldilocks: All the porridge bowls are full of your object. So are the chairs and beds. What will this intrusive tot do?

8. Hamlet: Instead of a skull, the Melancholy Dane is holding up your object. Imagine his speech to it. Imagine him trying to lift it, trying to keep hold of it, trying to remove the traces from his black velvet doublet.

9. Ichabod: The Headless Horseman is galloping down on poor Ichabod. Instead of a pumpkin, this time he is holding your object, ready to hurl it at Ichabod's head. What will happen?

10. Jack and Jill: These two kids have pails full of your object. They can barely get up the hill. See the pails overflow. See Jack and Jill try to keep them from spilling. What happens when they do?

By now you have realized that it isn't enough to imagine a ketchup bottle next to a bathtub or a postage stamp next to a toaster. In the peg system, the two objects must interact in some memorable way. Make it silly. Make it naughty. No one knows or cares what you are thinking. Come up with fanciful ways to relate two things, using the trillions of images stored in your Knowing Mind. Imagine bathing in ketchup. Imagine postage stamps stuck all over the toaster with giant stamps inserted in the slots instead of bread.

Another way to hook one thing to another is directly. Suppose you want to remember that the participants in a certain trade agreement were France, Poland, and China. You could imagine Polish sausage wrapped in a slice of French toast on a china plate. Or you want to remember that Mr. Blankensop's two children are named Frank and Alice. Imagine Frank Sinatra and Alice in Wonderland (or any other Frank and Alice you prefer) hoisting him on their shoulders. The next time you meet Mr. Blankensop, you can say, "And how are Frank and Alice?" He'll be impressed and never know about your image. Neither will Frank and Alice.

SOME MEMORY STORIES

Gou Yanling, a 26-year-old telephone operator in Harbin, China, demonstrated her skill at remembering phone numbers at a 1986 telecommunications meeting in Beijing. Gou, who had worked as an operator for five years, can remember 15,000 phone numbers: "I often memorize telephone numbers when I watch television, see advertisements, or pass shops and factories." She vowed to do better in the future, planning to add another 3,000 numbers before the next yearly conference, according to a report in the *San Francisco Chronicle.*

The world could use more Gou Yanlings, but even people with occasional memory lapses have contributions to make. Composer Ludwig von Beethoven was given a handsome horse by a grateful patron. Beethoven rode it several times, but then forgot all about it. The poor thing would have starved to death, except that a servant noticed its plight. The clever fellow rented the horse out, pocketed the fees, and some time later presented the overdue feed bills to a startled Beethoven. Obviously Beethoven could remember what he wanted to remember because, as we all know, he continued to compose complicated musical scores for years after he was deaf. He still heard the music in his head and transcribed the notes onto paper without the need to sound them out on a piano or clavier.

The point of each of these anecdotes is that both Gou and Beethoven were able to remember what was important to them. When we forget something, we never really got it in the first place; or it was misunderstood; or it was misfiled (like hearing the phrase "silver threads among the gold" and filing it under "fashion" instead of "song lyrics" or "old age").

If you suspect you are blocking yourself when you try to remember something "important," one part of your mind has probably placed a different value on its importance and is engaging in some subtle sabotage. Call your mental board into conference and explore why this particular thing may be provoking rebellion. As with all other projects, an executive order to remember will fail unless the entire mind agrees. Self-harassment only stiffens resistance and increases the memory block.

While you negotiate with yourself, don't forget:

- We remember best what enhances us and gives us pleasure.

- We tend to forget what doesn't influence or enrich our immediate lives.

- Anyone with a belly button is allowed at least a 20 percent margin for error in remembering.

Here's a story. Which part of the mind do you think is noticing?

The sunset beyond the coral reef was the most beautiful she had ever seen (1) _____. Victoria felt her heart pounding against her ribs (2) _____, her cheeks flushing with the joy of the moment (3) _____. The breeze teased her hair (4) _____ as it softly rustled the palm trees overhead, carrying the sound of distant singing (5) _____. "Only $3,995," she thought, "cheaper than last year's vacation and worth every penny (6) _____. Tomorrow, I must find out where the path along the cliff goes (7) _____. Oh, here comes Carlos! He's so good looking! (8) _____ It's all so lovely. I'm going to phone the office and tell them I'm staying another week (9) _____."

Answers

1. Knowing—the senses
2. Silent—physical response
3. Reacting—emotions
4. Knowing—the senses
5. Knowing—hearing
6. Organizing—evaluating
7. Wondering—curiosity
8. Knowing/Reacting/Organizing—seeing/emotions/ evaluating
9. Executive—decision

Would you care to predict what Victoria will be most likely to remember about her vacation in years to come?

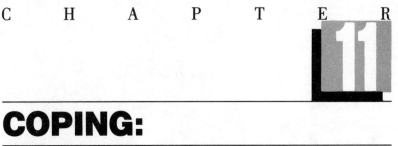

C H A P T E R 11

COPING:
STRESS, ANXIETY,
CRISIS, LOSS, ANGER,
DEPRESSION, PAIN

When you experience strong emotions, the elements of your mind are giving you some pretty powerful messages.

Stress: You may fail.
Anxiety: You may be hurt.
Crisis: You may die, spiritually or physically.
Loss: The world as you know it may cease to exist.
Anger: Something is awful. Fight it.
Depression: Everything is awful. Don't fight it.
Pain: You hurt!

These are all difficult and often overwhelming "states of mind," but it is interesting to note the differing *states* of the parts of the mind involved. Before you can experience stress or anxiety, the parts of the mind must *disagree* among themselves. But your entire mind must *agree* that there is a crisis or loss. Depression and anger, according to current theory, are the same feelings but projected inward for depression, outward for anger. Pain is your mind's interpretation of what's going on in your body.

To cope with stress or anxiety, the disputing parts of the mind need to come to an agreement. To cope with crisis, loss, anger, or depression, at least one part needs to disagree, to challenge the others about their evaluation of the situation until they collaborate to reframe the experience. Even with physical pain, the mind has some choices about how the body will experience the pain and respond to it.

STRESS

Stress and anxiety often seem to be the same thing and sometimes we go rapidly from one to the other, but there is a subtle difference. Both are internal sensations, possibly but *not necessarily* reacting to external happenings. However, stress is a resisting response, while anxiety is a flight response. That is, we push back against the pressure of stress, we pull away from the discomfort of anxiety.

WHAT IS STRESS?

The dictionary defines "stress" variously as emphasis, strain, load, force, pressure, resistance, tension, fear, and pain. Obviously we need some stress in our life in the sense of tension and stimulation. Otherwise we'd be mentally flabby and infinitely bored. Total lack of stimulation, such as solitary confinement, is considered a punishment. (There have even been recent studies noted by Ornstein and Sobel that suggest some cancers are promoted by feelings of boredom!)

Stress has developed into a catchall word and something of a bad guy. We hear a lot about the "stress of modern living," as if living in relatively good health to the average age of 70 is somehow more debilitating than the lives of our recent ancestors, half of whose children died in the first year of life, and who might themselves live to the ripe old age of 35—if they managed to avoid plague, cholera, smallpox, consumption, dropsy, brain fever, and the quinsy. Being an air traffic controller is certainly stressful. So was being a hunter or fisherman in the days when either your quest for food was successful or you and your family starved to death.

Whatever the internal or external justification for stress, it takes a definite physical toll on the body. The brain may alternately send out start and stop signals: Run! No, stop! No, *do* something! As

Ornstein and Sobel see it, the body is flooded with alternate chemical messages that really snafu the system. One hormone—norepinephrine—signals one set of nerve circuits centralized in the brain to start the heart pumping faster and restrict the smaller blood vessels, keeping the blood ready to supply the vital organs. The second hormone—acetylcholine—signals a decentralized nerve system all over the body to *resist* stress, to try to calm you down, slow your heart, deactivate key internal organs, increase deep breathing. When both hormones are activated at once, obviously your body faces a dilemma.

Primitive man could afford to flee every time something was just a little bit different. No doubt he wasted a lot of time running from shadows and blowing leaves, but he did survive to pass on his genes. Those who stopped to ponder the changes around them risked danger, even death. Modern man is bound by time limitations and social restrictions that don't allow for running from every real or potential threat. So we stew about what to do in such a situation. Is this really a threat? Shall I continue to act normal? Stay cool or react? And how?

Stress can make you sick. A study of first-year dental students by J. B. Jemmott, reported in *Lancet,* showed that students reported more colds following periods of high academic stress—a result that anyone who has attended school past kindergarten might have predicted. In *Hospital Practice,* H. Marowitz revealed that a nonsmoking male who experiences the stress of divorce is nearly as likely to die as a married man the same age who smokes a pack or more of cigarettes a day. Ulcers, high blood pressure, and strokes are all considered stress-related illnesses. Yet the mere presence of stress doesn't necessarily result in disease, any more than the mere presence of germs does. Most of us are remarkably capable of dealing with both as a rule. People *are* more likely to get sick when they feel they are under stress, but the connection is much more complex than that.

Usually when we say we are "run down" we mean we are feeling squeezed or stretched. People on vacation may race about more, sleep less, and eat erratically, yet they rarely complain that they are "stressed" or "burned out." The stimulation doesn't fit the profile of perceived stress.

You have probably seen those charts rating the stress of various happy and sad events in your life. Put together in the 1960s and presented in the *Journal of Psychosomatic Research,* they were based on questionnaires that asked people how much adjustment various significant personal events required. The most interesting aspect was that people felt positive occasions (marriage, promotions, buying a new house) required as much adjustment as negative occasions (illness, divorce, losing a job). The second most interesting aspect was that European and Japanese respondents ranked some events in quite different order from that of Americans.

For example, a jail term was ranked fourth on the American stress list but second by both Japanese and Europeans. Although the death of a spouse was number 1 on all lists, Americans rated it 100, the Japanese 108, but the Europeans only 66, using a scale in which marriage was the constant at 50. So the "reserved" Japanese either find getting married less stressful than Americans and Europeans do (accounting for the wide point spread), or the "more demonstrative" Europeans find losing a spouse much less stressful than do Americans and Japanese. Europeans rated pregnancy in sixth place (Americans, twelfth; Japanese, thirteenth) and the death of a close family member was fourth in Japan, fifth in America, but eighteenth in Europe. This might be because of the larger extended families common in Europe in which the loss of an aunt or uncle is a more common event, but the Japanese also have close and extensive family ties.

Are these cultural differences or just variables within the groups who filled out the questionnaires? Since all the ratings are highly subjective, perhaps trying to assign stress values to events should be regarded more as a guide than a gauge. Each event must be figured with the personal equation. For instance, losing one's mate is usually the ultimate sorrow, but Oscar Wilde spoke of the widow whose "hair had gone quite blonde with grief."

One thing the ratings didn't consider was the stress of *not* having things happen—of not getting married, not getting a job, not having a baby, not moving to a new home, not going to college. "Nonoccurence of desired events may be stressful," maintain Drs. Ornstein and Sobel, noting that "an unhappy marriage or poor working conditions are not really 'events' per se. . . ."

OUTCOME OF STRESS

Outside stress doesn't equal disease. Even great outside stress doesn't equal disease. To account for the obvious fact that some people survive appalling situations while others crumble at the first obstacle, Hans Selye divided stress into two kinds: "distress" from the Latin *dis* or bad, and "eustress" from the Greek *eu* or good.

Whether you decide to experience an outside situation as stress depends on a complex personal equation of four factors:

1. Its cumulative nature (type, frequency, duration, intensity)

2. Whether you see it as a threat or a challenge

3. Your current resources for dealing with it

4. Your current need for stimulation and excitement (arousal level)

STRESS IS A CHOICE

Stress is anything that we choose to interpret as outside pressure. We can choose to be oppressed or supported, hindered or advanced by this perceived force. We *choose* to be exhilarated or irritated by blaring horns, chirping birds, the various and often conflicting needs of people around us. Many people even seek out such stimulation deliberately, paying to have bright lights flashed in their eyes and 120-decibel music assault their eardrums, choosing the most highly spiced food, the fastest roller coasters and race cars, even precarious lifestyles. They interpret these stresses as stimulation and excitement.

What, then, is the cause of stress? When the parts of the mind disagree, stress is a common result. For instance, parents commonly feel pulled in several directions by the many demands of their children:

meeting of the minds

Executive Part: "I love my children."

Knowing Part: "They are being deliberately difficult while I try to read the newspaper."

Reacting Part: "I'm mad!"

Organizing Part: "The *Manual of Procedures* says you can't be mad at someone you love."

Reacting Part: (*feels guilty*)

Wondering Part: "What if I taped their mouths shut and tied them to a chair . . . "

Executive Part: "No, you can't! Grow up."

Wondering Part: "When's the next plane to Tahiti?"

Executive Part: (*like a stern schoolmaster*) "Behave yourself!"

TOO MUCH STRESS

Work situations provide many options for stress. We invest a lot of our own ego in performing well, meeting deadlines, responding confidently to requests, and appearing to do all this with unruffled ease. If we decide that the demands are unrealistic and just can't be met, we may respond like rats in a dead-end maze. We lose interest in trying. We get angry with others: "Who needs this crummy job anyway? No one could work with that bozo!" Or we get angry with ourselves; that is, we get depressed. (Being depressed at least gets rid of stress by getting all the factions of the mind to agree on something: "I'm a failure.")

Where there is a "boss," unrealistic scheduling can sometimes be negotiated and adjusted. When *you* are the boss, you furnish your own standards which can be far higher and more unattainable than anyone else's.

meeting of the minds

Executive Part: "Succeed!"
Wondering Part: "Define 'succeed.' "
Organizing Part: "You want success? I'll show you success! Your brother had better grades than you did. Your friend Joe makes more money than you do. Stan joined the company when you did and now he's a vice president."
Reacting Part: (*jealousy, fear, anger*)

At this point you can take a number of paths, depending on how the *Manual of Procedures* has dealt with this directive in the past.

EXCUSES FOR STRESS

Stress, like beauty, is in the mind of the beholder. You *choose* to respond with stress to an external or internal situation. Of course there are lots of situations that can correctly be called "stressful" because many people choose (or fail to reject) stress when they encounter them. Some popular "excuses" for stress are demanding jobs, family conflicts, not having enough money, difficult commutes, health problems, uncertainty about the future, being in a crowd, being alone, being young, being old, being smart, being stupid, being married, being single, being a man, being a woman. ("Stress" in response to fear of crime, illness, or war isn't actually stress, it's anxiety.)

Stress isn't a take-it-or-leave-it proposition. You don't either have to succumb to it or cut yourself off from the perceived source. The most difficult response is also the most successful: Reinterpret it. Reframe your response to the internal or external irritant.

Someone is constantly criticizing you?

Understand the personal weakness that causes him to do this. Feel sorry for him. Figure out how you can bolster his fragile ego so he will feel as good about himself as you feel about yourself. (Sure, some of the criticism may be justified—everyone can find something wrong if they look hard enough—but you're wise enough to pick out constructive comments from a stream of garbage and let the rest flow on down to the level where it belongs.)

Someone cuts you off on the highway?

Conjugation: I am rude conditionally.
You are rude deliberately.
All others are rude genetically.

Inner Voice	**Other Possibilities**
"Why am I such a failure?"	"Do I regard their achievements as success? Is a direct comparison possible? If so, what can I learn from their accomplishments?"
"What would happen if I harassed myself more?"	You furnish yourself with information about similar past attempts, evaluate them and decide they were counterproductive, come up with a new strategy.
"Maybe I should quit trying . . ."	"Maybe I should reconsider what kind of 'success' I want, what my talents and abilities and limitations are. . . ." Your mind produces a long list of achievements and skills. You decide to rewrite your *Manual of Procedures.*

Reverse this and think of ten reasons why others may be in such a hurry that they are forced to be rude. Make at least one of the reasons life-threatening and another one risqué. Do not respond with any part of your body or vehicle until you reach number ten. (This tactic works well for any encounter with rudeness—it provides you with valuable insights while you madden an actual boor with your soft, secret, knowing smile.)

> The neighbors play their stereo at night when I'm desperate for sleep. They do it just to make me mad.

Ignore their motivation. You don't have to psychoanalyze every unpleasantness. Concentrate on the sensation and weave it into the supportive messages you give yourself as you drift off to sleep. Wear earplugs if necessary. Experience the vibrations coming through the wall/floor/ceiling as the hum of a Rolls Royce Silver Cloud, purring over a silken ribbon of highway among the purple hills as the setting sun turns the clouds salmon, pink, lavender. . . . Find similar images to reframe flight delays, the dentist's chair, waiting lines, and traffic jams.

ANXIETY

According to some philosophers, anxiety is useful because it gets people to do things. If you feel you need anxiety to motivate yourself, that's okay. Skip to the next section. But if it gets in the way, stops you from doing things you want to do or performing as well as you know you can, then stay tuned.

Anxiety, like stress, is a self-manufactured, internal sensation. We may produce it in response to an external event, but the event doesn't *cause* anxiety. We perceive the event, interpret it, and then choose a response. "Nonsense," I can hear you saying, "when that cab almost ran me down, you can bet I had a reason to be anxious!"

Certainly you were upset. But fear cannot be experienced after the fact. You may have had the shakes as your body processed the rush of adrenaline pumped just before you leaped out of the way, but you were no longer anxious. Fear and anxiety are reserved for something that has not yet happened. If it hasn't happened yet, you still have a choice of responses. Even the skydiver who discovers her parachute is jammed and the earth is coming up to meet her awfully fast has choices about how she feels and how she acts.

Being aware of this freedom of choice is the first step to recognizing any sabotage by your emotions. Of course, if my best friend is critically ill or my house burns down, I will probably choose to feel terrible—to mourn—if only briefly, before summoning other emotions: empathy and support for the friend, excitement about rebuilding or finding a new place to live.

REPLACING ANXIETY WITH OTHER EMOTIONS

How can we choose emotions other than anxiety in response to common situations?

> I dread being in a group of new people, and usually avoid it. I get self-conscious. I can't remember anyone's name, feel really stupid, can't think of anything to say.

When we are very young, we notice everything and comment on it. As we mature, we start to sort information into patterns and learn to ignore what doesn't fit. We also learn not to comment on certain things: "Mr. Henderson smells bad." "Mommy's going wee-wee." "I hate Aunt Sue."

People who have trouble meeting new people often are listening to childhood messages: "It's not polite to notice." Sometimes, even, "It's *dangerous* to notice. You'll be punished." When we stop observing our external environment, it's easy to let our chemical system take over and concentrate on the internal—stepped-up heartbeat, a twinge in the stomach, the taste in our mouth as we try to untangle our tongue from our teeth. Keenly aware of the hair on the back of our necks, we assume that everyone else is scrutinizing us with the same intensity.

> I have to give a department progress report twice a year at the Chicago office. I know most of the guys there and I sure know the material, but I freeze up and make a mess of it.

When everyone is looking your way, it is natural to get a flood of adrenaline. In the caveman days this was the "fight or flight" mechanism that provided energy for either slugging it out or making a getaway.

This chemical wave is what provides performers and athletes with their natural energy for the task before them. It is a glorious sensation, even somewhat addictive—think of the ham actors, over-the-hill ballplayers, and second-rate politicians who are so reluctant to give up the spotlight.

But, interpreted as panic with nowhere to run, it can be disabling. Unless you use this flood of hormones, it may reduce you to a shivering, sweating, tongue-tied mess.

If you choose to feel trapped, your mental executive is quickly diverted from its purpose by wild and insistent reports of disaster down below. Sweating palms and an upset stomach overwhelm sales figures and statistics.

The first step for curing "stage fright" is to notice the rush of adrenaline you get before you even move from your seat to give your presentation. Immediately say, "Oh, good, I'm excited!" Without this chemical boost you would be flat. Interpreting this sensation as fear—scaring yourself—is absolutely optional.

Next, remember *what* you are eager for people to decide to do or believe as a result of your talk. Choose to adopt an attitude that says, "I'm here to help," rather than, "I want to seem important." Before you start speaking, really look at your audience. Establish rapport through eye contact. Here's where you begin the cycle of energy exchange between you and the group. Know what you want to say so well that your focus can be on how people are receiving your message. Turn to page 139-47 for helpful ways to remember what you want to say.

If you were taught "public speaking" some years ago, you may need to update your *Manual of Procedures* on speaking to groups. Some people were instructed to pick out a friendly face in the audience and focus on that person. This is deadly advice. It makes bored orphans out of everyone else. Worse yet is picking a spot slightly above the heads of the audience and focusing there while speaking. The audience is your power source. Nothing replaces the give-and-take of energy available to a speaker who knows the subject and develops the frame of mind that says, "I'm glad to be here. Let's have a good time delving into this subject."

FEAR OF FAILURE

One of the most common anxieties is fear of failure. Because anxiety is a "flight" mechanism, anxious people avoid doing something they're afraid they may not do well. A lot of people ask therapists to give them confidence. This is legitimate: If they don't feel competent, they probably won't use their skills well, even when they have the ability.

But what if they're really incompetent? Insecurity may be caused by a realistic evaluation of their own talents. If this is true, then confidence building will only produce false overconfidence, not increased ability. The confident person may be incompetent, but learns to hide it better.

Some famous people have made highly successful careers with only the image of competence. Grandiosity can be impressive when recognized, even occasionally endearing, but it is also dangerous. Periodically we read of people who have successfully posed as doctors, military or police officers, teachers, priests. They convinced themselves and others that they had a right to this prestigious position and power. Sometimes it was a deadly fraud. Other times it was a harmless fantasy. The "Great Impostor," Ferdinand Demara, Jr., who was the subject of a book and film biography, took many of these power fantasy roles, even performing surgery on critically injured sailors. Certain world leaders have enjoyed personal visions of omnipotence that cost the lives of millions of less inspired human beings.

Yet a little grandiosity, artfully employed, can be a source of growth. A visionary who describes a different world and inspires people to work toward that ideal is guilty of grandiosity, but we certainly don't equate Gandhi, Eleanor Roosevelt, or Martin Luther King, Jr., with Attila the Hun or Hitler.

Brief spurts of personal grandiosity, if wisely handled, can even provide instant energy for overcoming obstacles. Consider this anecdote reported by the *San Francisco Chronicle* in its obituary of Clare Boothe Luce. As a struggling young writer, she was turned down for a job by Conde Nast, owner of *Vanity Fair* and *Vogue* magazines. Nast then left for Europe. Luce plunked herself down at an empty desk and announced that she had been hired. By the time Nast returned six weeks later, she had proven herself. Three years later, she became managing editor of *Vanity Fair.*

THE MEDIOCRE APPROACH

Obviously somewhere between psychopathic grandiosity and crippling inferiority complexes is that oh-so-hard middle ground. ("Mediocre" originally meant *medium* or *middle,* not "less than good"!) Dare to be mediocre. Position your feet firmly on the middle ground. Always be willing to push yourself, to try new things, to stretch, to try side trips. Take risks. Make a fool of yourself. Be scared. But stop periodically for reality checks. Be ready to reframe your mission and goals to take advantage of your many real abilities, some newfound. You'll be more productive and more content.

DEFENSES AGAINST ANXIETY

Anxiety hurts. No wonder we want to run from it. Here are some other common defenses:

Denial or wishful thinking. The mental executive decides something is too disruptive to notice. The imagination provides seductive alternate scripts which all parts of the mind decide to accept. As psychologist Richard Lazarus says in *Psychology Today,* "Illusion can allow hope, which is healthy."

Reversal. When an anxiety is really strong, some people use it, like jujitsu, to do the opposite. They overcompensate. This can be constructive and a source of personal growth: learning to swim to overcome fear of the water; caring for a puppy to overcome fear of dogs. It can also be restricting: the person who fears his own appetites and becomes a rabid censor; the person who fears anything unfamiliar and becomes a zealous bigot.

Sublimation. Less extreme than reversal, sublimation consists of transforming or diverting disturbing impulses to more acceptable actions. You're furious so you scrub the floor or chop wood. You're sad so you go for a long walk. Every culture has developed a similar method for dealing with the various disruptive "vices" that mankind is so fond of—sex, alcohol, gambling, drugs, brawling, cheating on taxes, coveting this and that. One or two are chosen as "absolute must nots" and the rest are winked at. Alcohol and sex seem to be the key ingredients: if one is permitted, the other is not. Moslem culture bars alcoholic beverages but permits multiple wives. The Irish are very strict about sex, marry late, but embrace the "water of life."

Projection. We all use projection occasionally, transferring our fears and conflicts to someone else: "They always cheat, so why shouldn't I?" "Look at her pigging out on that cake." Again, extremes can be crippling: "He is (actually *I am*) stupid, rotten, hateful, crazy" or "They (actually *I*) despise, bore, disgust, infuriate me."

Some self-deception is essential to mental health. Too much is not only dangerous but addictive. These defenses can become so automatic we no longer realize we are using them; we lose control over them! Your job is: Know thyself . . . but not *too* well.

CRISIS

The definition of a crisis is an agreement of all parts of the mind that a crisis exists. It can be spilled milk or World War III. The most common crises are being in jeopardy or having a loved one in jeopardy, losing your job or source of income, illness, disaster, pestilence, flood, famine, war.

Amazingly, it is often easier to survive a crisis than low-level, day-to-day annoyances. Crisis has certain advantages: It is frequently shared with others; it is urgent, creating a heightened sense of awareness and energy; it is specific; it mobilizes.

POTENTIAL AND ACTUAL CRISIS

A potential crisis can produce anxiety and fear. We fear nuclear war. We fear getting cancer or a debilitating disease. We fear losing a loved one who is in danger, losing our job, losing our home as a forest fire advances toward it. What we *can't* fear or worry about is something that has already happened. It is over. We can only devise strategies for survival and recovery.

Let's look at the differences between potential and actual:

I may get fired. (anxiety, fear of failure)

Our company may go out of business. (anxiety, fear of loss)

I've been fired. (anxiety about the future, anger, chagrin, a sense of loss, a sense of failure, hope for the future)

Our company has gone out of business. (all of the above except chagrin, unless you identify strongly with the company's success and feel personally responsible for the failure)

Once you decide that a crisis exists (and it's possible though not usually profitable to ignore it), your mental executive begins problem-solving procedures. A crisis is simply a problem on a very large scale. It may involve reformatting your career, family structure, or life temporarily or permanently after catastrophic circumstances, but it is still a series of problems to be solved.

LOSS

Loss is a kind of problem too, but it lacks the detachment of increasing sales or getting a cat out of a tree. It is intensely personal, devastating, a violation of one's self. Loss makes us want to howl at the top of our lungs or shrivel into oblivion. Loss is death.

Loss can trigger a disruption of the body's immune system, part of our Silent Mind. Increased rates of infection, cancer, arthritis, and many other health problems seem to be related to lower immunity brought on by grief. Studies of recent widows and widowers have shown lower activity of "T-cells," the white blood cell that fights invaders. Ornstein and Sobel point out that the organs of immunity, the thymus gland, spleen, and the bone marrow, have receptors for chemicals that were thought to exist only in the central nervous system, and that damage to the brain can alter the immune function. Other studies indicate that a person's response—whether he fights back or gives up—affects his T-cell activity. Obviously the immune system responds to the workings of your conscious mind, even though you may not be conscious of it.

There is no solution for loss, only strategies for healing. Grieving is a traditional method, out of fashion for a time, but now gaining new respect. Grieving involves the entire mind.

The mental executive recognizes the loss. Then it abdicates control, however briefly, while the other parts of the mind respond.

The wondering part poses the big question, "Why me?!" followed quickly by, "What if I . . ." or "If only I . . ." It creates little scenarios that rewrite history with happier endings. It projects further calamities. It seeks answers where there may be none. In extreme cases, the Wondering Mind can take over and block out the loss with psychoses or amnesia. Healing begins when the wondering part of your mind turns to questions about your welfare. What can be done? How can you survive? Recover? Make things better?

Your organizing ability occupies itself with repetitions and rituals. Rituals are essential for beginning the healing process. A funeral is a ritual to begin healing after death. Buying new clothes is a ritual, often associated with spring, to symbolize renewal. Holidays and ceremonies are times of renewal. Connecting with the meaningful things of the past is stabilizing. Feeling part of a cycle instead of a finality is consoling.

The emotional reacting part of your mind hurts. Sorrow may be mixed with fear of the future, anger at the loss, depression, guilt for not doing more to prevent the loss. The healing element of your emotions is love—love for others that distracts it from its own pain, and love for self that, over time, lets it nurture and restore itself.

Through all this your senses, the knowing part of the mind, experience a general shutdown. Colors are dimmer. Food has no taste. Once-important things seem meaningless. This temporary turning down the dial on awareness also lowers the volume on pain. Bright, urgent images of what has been lost occasionally blot out the present reality. Healing begins when the vivid past and the gray present slide toward each other and merge in a common ground. Healing is complete when the painful past recedes and the present becomes foreground again. The images of the past are always there to comfort us but they no longer hurt or overwhelm the present.

Finally the mental executive takes charge again, supervising the healing process and offering suggestions and occasionally orders.

MOURNING LOSS

Donna wanted help ten years after her divorce because she realized she was still strongly affected by her loss. Her husband had been an alcoholic, and she had decided to make a separate life for herself and her children. It had been a good life. She was proud of her success as a provider and parent, and had almost forgotten about her ex-husband. Then he remarried. She was astonished at how shocked and depressed the news made her.

When mourning is delayed, sometimes a therapist is the catalyst to resolve blocks and complete the process. Redecision therapist Dr. Robert Goulding asked Donna how she felt about her ex-husband. She seemed to have little reaction. Then he asked her what her *Manual of Procedures* said about marriage in general. She came to life, responding warmly with a detailed, idealized description of a perfect home life: love, contentment, children, two adults growing together and growing old together. This *Manual of Procedures* image was what she was mourning, not the remarriage of her husband. She felt angry that she had lost this "birthright," that her life had been "wasted."

"How will you complete the mourning process for the perfect marriage?" he asked. She decided that she would like to hold a symbolic funeral. She would no longer mourn her "failure," but the loss of the fantasy. She did so by imagining a coffin full of all the old images of the perfect home—spotless laundry, steaming pies, ruffled curtains, white picket fences. She imagined nailing the lid on, then watching it being lowered into the ground. She tossed pretend dirt on it. Then she held an imaginary "wake" with tea and cookies and happy talk about the possibilities ahead. All this was done with a playful, mocking air, but there was a seriousness underneath. A fantasy had been laid to rest and she was free to celebrate the reality of her past and future successes.

MOURNING FOR WHAT IS NOT LOST

Another kind of mourning, one that is becoming more common in this age of two-career families, is loss of identity through the loss of a job. Marion had gotten her doctorate degree and achieved tenure at a major university where her husband also taught. Her life revolved around the stimulation of her classroom and the status it gave her. Then her husband was asked to become department head at another school a thousand miles away. Being a "good wife," she automatically urged him to accept, and they set off to start a new life. At first Marion could only get a part-time teaching job at a local college. As a part-timer, she found she was considered an outsider. She had gone from being a valued spokesperson and team member to having her opinions ignored at faculty meetings.

When Marion came to me, she just knew that she was hurting, but didn't know precisely why. Part of fixing something broken is figuring out what is different now than when the thing was working. We quickly established that she was still mourning the good feelings she had had about herself in her former highly responsible position. In a sense, she had lost her self, a self that was competent, respected, successful. Her marriage, alone or in combination with her new, less prestigious job, was not providing enough opportunities for her to continue her old identity.

Some losses are irreversible. Others are not. Neither Marion nor her potential for self-fulfillment had ceased to exist. Instead of helping her to grieve, I encouraged Marion to create a list of her options. Once she recognized them, she was ready to begin problem solving instead of mourning. Here is the list she made:

- I can continue as I am doing and be miserable.

- I can continue as I am doing and be happy by reframing my expectations and needs. I could replace the fulfillment I got from my tenured position with fulfillment from what I have now—trying to get more gratification from marriage, feeling part of the marriage team, working to reestablish myself careerwise.

- I can go back to my former position, or at least to the same university where people know and respect me. This might mean abandoning marriage and acknowledging that marriage alone can't provide me with an identity.

- I can try to build a new career identity here that includes marriage.

- I can try to build a new career identity here that excludes marriage.

Just having a list of options gave Marion a new sense of control. Part of her mourning had been caused by her sense of helplessness. (Helplessness breeds desperation and rebellion. Anyone who feels trapped and hopeless is likely to see fewer options and perhaps to react in irrational or unproductive ways.) When Marion realized that she had choices, healing had begun.

ANGER

Few people are neutral about anger. We speak of "righteous wrath" and the "wrath of the Lord," but *Wrath* (or sometimes *Anger*) was also one of the Seven Deadly Sins. Anger has certain admirable functions—it gets the adrenaline pumping, it gets attention, it drives away predators, it may release tension. However, today's world seems to have outgrown the need for displays of anger. Constant anger, called "hostility," is seen as counterproductive, disruptive, negative, a health risk: "Hostility tears the social fabric. . . ."

Forgetting about others for the moment, what effect does anger have on the angry person? Once upon a time it aided survival by frightening off potential enemies. Today some studies show that hostile behavior actually aids survival in nursing homes. Pleasant, agreeable "good guys" seem to die quickly after making the transition to an institutional setting. According to Ornstein and Sobel the people most likely to stay alive are "aggressive, irritating, narcissistic, and demanding." Long-term survivors of breast cancer have been found to be far more negative than short-term survivors. The report in the *Journal of the American Medical Association* says they had significantly higher scores for hostility, guilt, and depression, and were frequently angry with their doctors and their treatment. They often let others know they were distressed. Before you decide that it's a good thing to blow your top, consider a host of other studies showing that a negative attitude lowers immunity and increases the incidence of many diseases.

There's a lot of scientific literature on the bad effects of *sup*pressing anger and also on *ex*pressing it. Anger causes a quick jolt of adrenaline to hit the bloodstream, constricting thousands of blood vessels as the heart tries to compensate with quick, hard contractions. Anger is a common culprit, or at least the outward sign of internal distress, in cardiovascular and coronary disease.

The term "Type A behavior" describes a person characterized by an urgent sense of time, devotion to work, excessive hostility, denial of fatigue, and competitiveness. These Type As, unless persuaded to change their ways, seem to topple over at an early age. The reference *Anger and Hostility in Cardiovascular and Behavioral Disorders* reports that they are twice as likely as otherwise similar men to have coronary artery disease. A revealing example of a Type A self-evaluation is offered by Ornstein and Sobel:

> I do not believe that I have excess hostility; this is
> due in part to the fact that my intellectual, physical,
> cultural, and hereditary attributes surpass those of
> 98 percent of the bastards I have to deal with.
> Furthermore those dome-head fitness freak, goody-
> goody types that make up the alleged 2 percent are no
> doubt faggots anyway, whom I could beat out in a
> second if I weren't so damn busy fighting every
> minute to keep that 98 percent from trying to walk
> over me. To answer your question, however, if I could
> curb my inate [sic] modisty [sic], humility and
> empathy for my fellow man, perhaps. . . .

Type As don't outperform calmer Type Bs, but they have some initial advantages over them. Because they perform at such high speed, they may get off to a faster start in the earlier part of their career. They impress the boss. But as they advance up the ladder, their hasty, simplistic decisions and hostility toward others become liabilities when they need to negotiate and do long-range planning. (When a Type A recognizes the disadvantages of this behavior and wants to become a more complex, wider-ranging Type B, he wants to reach this goal *immediately.*)

So if suppressing anger can make you sick and expressing anger can make you sick, is there an alternative? Fortunately there is. First, let's debunk the "teakettle theory" of anger: that there's a "steam pressure" that has to go somewhere. Anger, like joy and boredom, is an optional response, even to extreme provocation. You don't have a healthy quota of *boredom* inside you, straining to get out. Controlling anger doesn't necessarily mean suppressing it. You can also eliminate it. Drs. Bernie Zilbergeld and Arnold Lazarus, authors of *Mind Power: Getting What You Want through Mental Training*, have found that ". . . people who learn to control or manage their anger suffer no negative consequences; on the contrary, they are invariably much happier, more satisfied, and more productive." Their view is shared by Carol Tavris in her book *Anger: The Misunderstood Emotion*.

So . . . your alternative is to reframe anger into a more productive response. More productive for you. More productive for those around you. And more productive for what you want to accomplish. Some reframing exercises are at the end of this chapter. Until you learn this valuable skill, you are in the position of the influential eighteenth century English physician Dr. John Hunter, who said, "My life is in the hands of any rascal who chooses to annoy me." Dr. Hunter died following a heated discussion at a board meeting at St. George's Hospital in London.

DEPRESSION

Our ancestors knew what they were doing when they fought depression with "good, hard work." Depression may or may not be anger turned inward, but it is definitely an agreement of all parts of the mind that life is awful, hopeless, the pits. Rigorous mental exercise distracts us into noticing new things, gets us to stop counting miseries and start organizing other information.

Vigorous physical exercise accelerates the heart rate and breathing, increases the amount of oxygen in the blood and releases norepinephrine to the brain, and—the big payoff—blocks depression. A study by University of Kansas psychologists, reported in the *Journal of Personality and Social Psychology,* confirmed several previous studies, finding that "the subjects in the aerobic exercise condition evidenced reliably greater decreases in depression than did subjects in the placebo condition or subjects in the no-treatment condition."

While the release of norepinephrine helps block depression, the increased oxygen to the brain and the "psychosocial" stimulation that occurs in many exercise situations may also energize one or more of the minds. Since depression requires a united front, it only takes one backslider noticing new options to overthrow the life-is-rotten regime.

Some strategies for dealing with depression are:

Withdraw. Don't deal with difficult issues when you are depressed. Set aside a few minutes to sit and really focus on how horrible you feel. Imagine your toes, your knees, your hips all deep in blue, soggy depression. Then see your body, your arms, your neck cold and wet. Finally the blues totally engulf you, closing over your head. Savor the immersion in this quivery blue environment (choose another color if you really like blue). After a few minutes (if you can sustain your mood that long), notice how hard it is to keep up this intensity. Let the depression slide away in reverse order. Or maybe it changes color, taking on a warm glow. You are now ready for one of the following steps.

Share. Mention to someone supportive that you have had a rotten day. Don't dwell on it, just get it out. Then go on to lighter topics. (Bartenders and therapists are good listeners, but friends and relatives are cheaper and often just as good.)

Pretend. Put on a brightly colored outfit, dance, tell jokes, sing, jump up and down. Put on a false face of merriment. Often it turns the tide. A study at the University of California at San Francisco, discussed in *Approaches to Emotion: A Book of Readings*, edited by Klaus Scherer and Paul Ekman, showed that you can call up different emotions by changing your expression. Psychologist Paul Ekman asked people to make faces, raising and lowering eyebrows and lips. People consistently experienced emotions that matched their facial image. So, when your heart is aching, a happy face can cheer you up. If it doesn't, at the very least you'll be able to come up with some wonderfully ironic poetic images for your autobiography.

Reward yourself. No need to indulge yourself with a 1,000-calorie sundae or a $5,000 wardrobe, unless you can afford them. But you might consider a movie or sauna, some bubble bath, a bunch of daisies, a new box of paper clips, a few extra minutes at coffee break or in the shower or with the morning paper.

Do a kindness. Plan something nice for someone else. This is usually the last thing on your mind. That's why it is invaluable. Getting your Knowing Mind to notice and pay attention to someone else is a good way to start the rebellion that ends depression.

Do something physical. Run, jog, walk. Deliberately drop a file folder or handful of rubber bands and then pick up all the pieces one at a time, bending from the waist. Rearrange your possessions. (Leave other people's alone!) Even if you're in traction or a wheelchair, there are still parts of your body you can exercise. Roll your eyes, make faces, wiggle your ears and anything else that will move.

Plan. Even if you're so low you could walk on stilts under a dachshund, focus on doing one thing later today that is pleasurable. Arrange to meet a friend. Phone someone interesting. Have something special for dinner. Get your Organizing Mind to construct lists of potential pleasures.

Write it down. One of the valuable things about keeping a diary is learning that nothing is permanent. Some people think whatever they write is carved in stone. I help my writing classes realize that just the opposite is true. Sorrow, pain, happiness, elation—all come and go. When you are depressed, you feel as though you have always been depressed and will remain that way forever. But nothing is forever, even depression.

PAIN

Pain is sometimes optional. Think twice before living with pain. Maybe you don't have to. Pain is an alert system, a language of the body. Masking it with painkillers can be like turning off the smoke detector so you're not bothered by the beep. On the other hand, enduring pain without exploring options is defeat.

PAIN: GOOD OR BAD?

Pain has a long tradition of nobility. In the Old Testament, Job is a powerful role model for enduring. People are told to stop sniveling, take it like a man, take your medicine, don't be a whiner, no pain-no gain. Pain is used as a punishment. Flagellants seek spiritual benefits by whipping themselves. Sometimes children who are spanked or beaten begin to look forward to the external pain as a cure for the inner tension of guilt. Sadomasochists actively seek out pain for the pleasure and release it brings. Obviously pain can elevate the other senses and occasionally act as a source of emotional energy and insight. Saki, in the play *Teahouse of the August Moon,* quotes an Asian proverb, "Pain makes men think; thought makes men wise."

Despite some benefits, pain is usually regarded as negative and destructive. Unrelieved, it can incapacitate and trigger fear, anxiety, and depression. Some depression in older people comes from all those unfamiliar aches and pains—not that we hurt significantly more than we did 20 or 40 or 60 years ago, but that there seems to be less chance of quick and total relief.

Doctors, like everybody else, are ambivalent about pain. Pain is a valuable clue to injuries and diseases, but stopping pain is one of their professional goals. Some will try to zap every twinge with pills. Others will smilingly urge patients to "learn to live with it." And how many times have you heard, "This won't hurt," just before it does? Pain is complicated because no one can ever know what someone else is feeling and because psychic pain is so inevitably and inscrutably entwined with pain from purely physical causes.

DEALING WITH PAIN

The first step to overcoming pain is to try to identify the cause and treat it. Your mind notices and runs through its repertory of ways to deal with the pain. These may be simple or sophisticated, depending on the information you have accumulated. You then decide on a course of action, anything from taking the weight off your feet to choosing from several proposed medical treatments.

Even with access to the most informed and skilled medical care and with the brightest, happiest personal attitude, everyone sooner or later is subjected to some kind of physical discomfort that can't be ignored. When you really *do* have to live with such a situation, here are some strategies for you to use:

Get excited. Being involved in something that calls on all parts of the mind leaves little brain power to pay attention to pain.

Relax. Some pain is caused by or aggravated by muscle tension. Practice taking deep breaths and stretching during the day. Set aside time for complete physical relaxation in which you systematically tense and release all your muscles. Allow yourself to daydream periodically. Letting the parts of your mind drift can be as good a tonic as a massage.

Reframe the sensation. Discomfort that is perceived as fixing something is more easily tolerated—dental braces for instance, or the itching that signals healing. So-called "natural" childbirth works in two ways. It uses education to eliminate much of the painful tension produced by fear of the unknown. It also helps the mother experience and work *with* the muscular contractions as they maneuver the baby through the birth canal in powerful and intricate interaction.

Laugh. Despite all the cliches about laughter being the best medicine, there is simply no way to laugh and concentrate on hurting at the same time. Seek out cheerful companions, witty books, funny films, droll conversations. Humor is not just a distraction from pain, it is an antidote.

HARDINESS

Who are the people who survive all the hard stuff that life throws at them? What characteristics do they have? What are the characteristics of their situation in life? Medicine and science usually study people who succumb to stress, anxiety, pain, and the rest, but fortunately they sometimes look at the survivors.

IN CONTROL

One thing we have discovered is that unpleasant job demands such as noise, heat, physical exertion, and repetitive work don't themselves cause heart disease. But these high demands do cause problems when combined with a sense of not being in control—of having little say over the rate of work or access to supports. This is called having little "job latitude."

Not being able to control stressful occurrences can lead to what psychologist Martin Seligman calls "learned helplessness," which goes along with loss of self-confidence, poorer performance, and health problems. Feeling in control reduces stress. A group of top business executives were asked to name the most stressful factors in their jobs. Although their jobs involved a lot of responsibility, they reported they felt very little stress. Apparently being able to control things means we can tolerate a much bigger load. It's no wonder that most orchestra conductors enjoy such surprising longevity. This is understandable. They have total, dictatorial control over many bright, talented people, and they use all parts of their mind to the fullest, organizing, creating, planning, and experiencing intense emotion.

For the average worker, just being able to phone home during the day—which is prohibited on some jobs—is a valuable personal support. Other job supports might include setting your own schedule, being able to ask for and get help easily, even being able to participate in the company decision process. A study of Swedish workers reported in *Social Science and Medicine* suggested that the best work combination in terms of health combines medium job demands with high opportunities to adjust to the demands.

HAVING COHERENCE

Another factor in functioning happily in a less-than-perfect world is seeing your surroundings as understandable, logical, and controllable. In his book *Health, Stress, and Coping*, Israeli medical sociologist Aaron Antonovsky calls this "coherence." The conditions we need to encounter (or create through selection and possibly reframing) are demands that are:

- Understandable—we see that demands are clear, predictable, consistent.

- Manageable—we have access to the necessary resources to meet demands.

- Meaningful—we feel demands of living are worth investing in and committing to, are worthwhile challenges rather than threats or unwelcome burdens.

HAVING FRIENDS

People who aren't connected to other people seem more vulnerable. Statistically, you are two or three times more likely to die if you are single, separated, divorced, or widowed, according to Ornstein and Sobel. You are also five to ten times more likely to be hospitalized for mental problems. If you are pregnant, you are more likely to have complications if you rate low on perceived emotional

support, says a report in the *American Journal of Epidemiology.*
Even if you're isolated from other humans, researchers have discovered
what pet owners have known for a long time: dogs (and cats and
canaries and goldfish) are man's best friends. The study in *Public
Health Reports* says that heart attack victims who owned pets were
five times more likely to be alive a year later than those without pets.
At first glance, you might think that the pet owners were responding
to the light exercise of daily dog walks, but even those with fish,
birds, and reptiles benefited. One theory is that talking to an animal
or watching a tank full of fish is soothing and lowers blood pressure.
Also, being responsible for another life can make us more eager to
survive ourselves.

HAVING YOUR EXPECTATIONS MET

Knowing what is expected of you—having a realistic picture of
what needs to be done—and then pacing yourself accordingly is a
big factor in hardiness. In a study reported in *American Health,*
Israeli soldiers on a march were divided into four groups. All the
groups marched the same distance, 40 kilometers or about 25 miles,
but each was given different directions.

Group One was told the exact distance. During the march they
were told periodically how far they had come and how much farther
they had to go. Group Two was told "this is the long march you heard
about," but they were never told how long the march would be nor
how far they had come. Group Three was told they would march 30
kilometers. When they had marched that distance, they were told
they must march another 10 kilometers. Group Four was told that
they would march 60 kilometers, but were stopped after 40 kilometers.

All four groups marched the same distance with their feet, but
their heads viewed the experience quite differently. Group One,
which had realistic information, had the fewest drop outs and
showed the least amount of stress. Group Two, which had no
information, showed the most stress. These soldiers were also the
least successful at guessing how far they had already marched, both
overestimating and underestimating the distance by wide margins.
Group Three, the one told the march was 30 kilometers and then
told to march another 10 kilometers, became very discouraged but
finished the march. Group Four, told they had to go 60 kilometers,

was completely demoralized. Many soldiers in this group dropped out after 10 kilometers. Even stopping after "only" 40 kilometers didn't improve the men's morale. Unfortunately life is not always fair. Situations are bound to come up in which our original concept of a job must be drastically changed. This is where the more abstract concept of being in control of one's life is very useful. It allows much more flexibility in adjusting to fluctuating demands and goals.

HAVING RESOURCES

Your car breaks down in a snowstorm and you are standing at the side of the road. Your degree of distress should be directly related to your degree of resources to solve the problem. If you are warmly dressed, with a $20 bill in your pocket and empty taxis streaming by, your distress level is likely to be low. If you are scantily dressed and there is no one around for miles, your level will be high. The money, warm clothes, and available taxis are physical resources, some of which you are directly responsible for (money, warm clothes) and one of which (the empty cabs) you are not. Resources can be emotional too. We've all had moments when we say, "I just can't deal with that now!" The frequency and intensity of such moments is an indicator of personal resources. Social connections in the form of family, friends, community, country are another form of resources. When menaced by pre-World War I international villains, the heroine of Terence Rattigan's play, *The Sleeping Prince,* dismisses them airily: "You can't do anything to *me. I'm* an American." Her insouciance gets a laugh, but it typifies the sense of being part of a protective, supportive, even charmed group.

People with hardiness and resilience seem to possess similar qualities. A study of 700 American Telephone & Telegraph executives showed that the ones who seemed to experience the least stress and stress-induced illness showed a strong commitment to themselves, their work, and their family. The report, described in *Hardy Executive: Health Under Stress* by Salvatore R. Maddi and Suzanne C. Kobasa, disclosed that they had strong values and possessed a sense of control over their lives. They also had the ability to see change as a challenge rather than a threat.

Another study of 72 children who were born and raised in chronic poverty and reared by mothers with little education sought to understand how these children survived overwhelming odds to become happy, confident, competent adults. In *Vulnerable but Invincible: A Study of Resilient Children,* Emmy E. Werner and Ruth S. Smith reported that these children shared certain qualities. They were "socially responsive" and active even when very young and related well to others. They were responsible, achievement-oriented, positive, found (or made) coherence in their lives, and were able to draw on a number of informal resources of support. Their interests were not limited by their gender. They all were eager to "improve themselves" and had a strong sense of self.

Although many of their mothers worked, these children had had extensive contact with their mothers during the first year of life. After that they were often cared for by other family members and formed strong bonds with them. Many lived in homes with several generations. Their families shared the same values and they had many family members to turn to for support and advice in times of crisis.

HAVING FLEXIBILITY

When low-hardiness people lose their jobs or face another major change, they see it as a catastrophe. When high-hardiness people have similar experiences, they tend to see it as an expected risk and an opportunity to do better. Ornstein and Sobel note that, "Hardy people transform problems into opportunities and thereby do not elicit a stress response in the first place."

Hardy people are aware of how much stimulation they need to function best, and are skilled at adjusting it to their current needs. They choose environments that are most likely to match their needs. They also value change, interpreting it as provocative rather than disorderly. Finally, hardy people seem to know when to be flexible and when to be stubborn, when to sit tight and when to act. They seem to be more skilled than others at selecting the most productive response because they have a strong sense of who they are and where they want to go.

How do you usually respond to these common situations? It's okay to check more than one answer. Do you have choices about this response?

	Pleasure	Embarrassment	Anger	Resentment	Sorrow	Fear	Little or No Response
1. A stranger compliments you on your appearance.	☐	☐	☐	☐	☐	☐	☐
2. A good friend criticizes you.	☐	☐	☐	☐	☐	☐	☐
3. You lose a treasured memento due to the carelessness of a family member.	☐	☐	☐	☐	☐	☐	☐
4. A stranger shouts at you angrily on the street.	☐	☐	☐	☐	☐	☐	☐

	Pleasure	Embarrassment	Anger	Resentment	Sorrow	Fear	Little or No Response
5. Your boss criticizes your fellow employees and holds you up to them as a good example.	☐	☐	☐	☐	☐	☐	☐
6. Another car cuts you off on the highway.	☐	☐	☐	☐	☐	☐	☐
7. Someone cuts in front of you in line.	☐	☐	☐	☐	☐	☐	☐
8. You hear a strange noise in the middle of the night.	☐	☐	☐	☐	☐	☐	☐
9. A snowstorm blocks all the roads and you can't get to work.	☐	☐	☐	☐	☐	☐	☐
10. Someone is ill and you have to take over their duties.	☐	☐	☐	☐	☐	☐	☐

How aware are you of your emotions? How do they color your thinking?

Happy. List five things that you usually respond to with joy or pleasure:

1.

2.

3.

4.

5.

Sad. List five things that you usually respond to with sorrow, tears, a sense of loss.

1.

2.

3.

4.

5.

Anger. List five things that you usually respond to with anger.

1.

2.

3.

4.

5.

Fear. List five things that you usually respond to with fright.

1.

2.

3.

4.

5.

Excitement. List five things that you usually respond to with a sense of curiosity and energy.

1.

2.

3.

4.

5.

Contentment. List five things that you usually respond to with a sense of comfort and calm.

1.

2.

3.

4.

5.

Love. List five things that you usually respond to with a warm sense of intimacy and affection.

1.

2.

3.

4.

5.

Go back over your list and check any of your responses that you would like to change. Write an alternate response to the occasion in the margin. We'll refer to this list when we get to "cues" in chapter 13—how you can decide to use the occasion to cue an entirely different response.

Note: While the emotional part of the mind provides us with a fear response to selected stimuli, it can also be valuable and effective in blocking uncomfortable messages. If we actively feared everything that could and will go wrong, we would probably come to a standstill. Our own mortality is a good example. But this blocking is very tricky. The certainty that "It can't happen to me" contributes to auto accidents, teenage pregnancy, alcoholism, chemical dependency, cancer from smoking or chewing tobacco, and the initial apathy over AIDS.

How much control do you have over your body's physical responses? Try these exercises in consciously experiencing your body.

1. Don't change position. Focus on your body. What part of your body is the most tense? What part is the most relaxed? Can you relax the tense part by conscious effort? Can you tighten the relaxed part by conscious effort?

2. Stretch. Tense all your muscles, raise your arms, extend your legs, reach as far as you can. How does it feel? What feels good? What doesn't?

3. Now take a deep breath. Again. How does it feel? What feels good? What doesn't?

4. When you're under pressure, does part of your body start hurting? Headache, stomachache, stiff neck? Try to reexperience that sensation now. Then try to make the sensation come and go until you recognize how to control it.

5. The next time you feel pretty good about your thought processes— you're working efficiently, solving problems comfortably, just taking things in stride—stop a moment and analyze how your body feels. Exhilarated? Energized? Does your body seem to change in some way? Does it seem to disappear altogether, leaving just your mind? What do you think of these impressions? Do you want to change them? Do you think duplicating these sensory impressions could help you reexperience your high efficiency level?

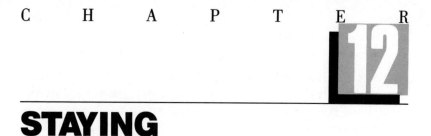

C H A P T E R

12

STAYING
SMART

One day in ancient Greece, a scholar named Aristotle noticed that women and slaves were often able to do things that he couldn't do. (He had a lot of time to think about such things because the women and slaves did most of the work.)

Aristotle tried to come up with a theory to explain this. His older contemporary, Plato, had already suggested that the intellect was separate from the body and its practical skills. So Aristotle took this idea one step further, deciding that theoretical thinking was separate from and—since he did a lot of it—superior to practical thinking.

The idea that there are two separate kinds of thinking, abstract and concrete, the one somehow better than the other, curiously became one of the basic beliefs of action-oriented western civilization. Aristotle created such a reverence for the theory that it was two thousand years before anyone actually tested some of his scientific theories and proved them right or wrong. We still refer to certain studies as the "liberal arts" because they were the domain of *free* men, while the fine and mechanical arts were left to artisans who were chiefly slaves. Practical people still smirk at impractical "ivory tower" thinkers, while theorists disdain what they consider the restricted mentality of the practical. Psychologist Rudolf Arnheim writes in *Visual Thinking* that "the middle class handles chiefly symbols . . .

the working class handles chiefly things."

Another popular myth about intellect is that it decreases as we get older, until inevitably, like Shakespeare's aged pantaloon, we settle into "second childishness and mere oblivion." Until this century that was often true, but, with today's tremendous advances in nutrition and medicine, many of us will keep our wits about us into our nineties and even beyond. In this chapter we'll look at several studies that indicate it is possible to maintain and even restore intellectual functioning in our later years. But first, let's look at what intelligence is and isn't.

INTELLIGENCE

What is intelligence? "We use [the word] so often," says Harvard psychologist Howard Gardner, "that we have come to believe in its existence, as a genuine tangible, measurable entity, rather than as a convenient way of labeling some phenomena that may (but may well not) exist." Gardner also notes that "reason, intelligence, logic, [and] knowledge are not synonymous. . . ."

Despite constant scrutiny and evaluation, no one has been able to come up with a generally accepted idea of what intelligence is. Here are a few definitions to choose from:

- Capacity for reasoning, understanding, and for similar forms of mental activity; aptitude in grasping truths, facts, meanings, etc. (*Random House Dictionary*)

- The ability to carry on abstract thinking. (L. M. Terman)

- The ability to adapt oneself to relatively new situations in life. (R. Pintner)

- The capacity to learn or to profit by experience. (W. F. Dearborn)

- The capacity for knowledge and knowledge possessed. (V. A. C. Henmon)

- Learning to adjust to one's environment, the capacity to get along well in all sorts of situations. (S. S. Colvin)

- [It] allows us to anticipate ill consequences without suffering them. (R. Peters)

- The elements usually measured by our tests, [and] certain other types of capacity which they measure scarcely at all. (F. N. Freeman)

- A recording mechanism and something to record. (B. R. Buckingham)

Psychologist Daniel Keating comments drolly in *Advances in the Study of Human Intelligence* that "We who study [intelligence] formally have the primary right to define it, and hence usually end up having more of it than other groups. . . ."

THE FIRST IQ TESTS

All of us have taken tests to rate our Intelligence Quotient (IQ). But what is an IQ? What *do* intelligence tests test? How valid are all those numbers so prized by educators, employers, and social clubs for geniuses? And does an IQ have any relation to our ability to think and function as adults?

The first formalized intelligence tests were developed for children. At the beginning of the twentieth century, French educator Alfred Binet, with his colleague Théodore Simon, looked for a way to assign children to the appropriate grade level and to identify retarded children so they could receive extra help. Binet came up with the idea of figuring a child's "mental age."

Since all children operate at different levels in different areas, he contrived questions covering as much ground as possible: In *The Mismeasure of Man,* Stephen J. Gould quotes Binet as saying, "It matters very little what the tests are, so long as they are numerous." To create his tests, Binet asked groups of children to answer sample questions. When 65 percent in a particular age group got a question right, it went into the test for that age. (It is intriguing that there are always some questions younger children do better on than older children. These are dropped from the tests.)

When a child can answer most of the questions assigned to the test for a given age, that test-age represents his or her "mental age." The Intelligence Quotient is figured by comparing the mental age with the physical age:

$$IQ = \frac{\text{Mental Age}}{\text{Physical Age}} \times 100$$

For instance, a seven-year-old who scores like a five-year-old would have an IQ of $5/7 \times 100$, or 71. A seven-year-old who scores like a nine-year-old would have an IQ of $9/7 \times 100$, or 129. This measurement is *comparative* (one person compared to others in the same group) rather than *absolute* (one person compared to a fixed, unvarying point), so the 100 of ten or 20 years ago can be quite different from the 100 of today. If some unforeseen calamity—massive famine, a viral epidemic, video games—suddenly resulted in massive mental retardation in all eight-year-olds, their *average* intelligence would then become the norm for that age group—an IQ of 100—and the tests adjusted accordingly.

An IQ test tests the potential ability of a child to do well in a traditional *academic setting*. Having established a way to measure this potential, Binet stopped short of theorizing about what it was that he was measuring. Until recently, everyone has been eager to test intelligence, but few have been eager to define it.

IQ TESTS FOR ADULTS

IQ tests were designed to select the best grade for each child. Then, when World War I came along, officials wanted an easy, "scientific" way to screen large numbers of enlistees. Binet's test was adapted, and the group IQ test for adults was born. Suddenly everyone became IQ conscious.

But this nice, neat way to classify human beings soon presented new questions. For instance, identical twins sometimes have IQ scores 20 points apart. Also, improving a child's environment can raise his or her IQ score over 30 points. And then, as psychologist Roger Peters says, " . . . learning to learn blurs the traditional distinction between innate capacity and learned contents. . . . " We can learn to be smarter.

Understandably, the IQ scale is questionable when applied to adults. How much more intelligent is a 40-year-old than a 35-year-old? Is someone 80 years old twice as smart as someone who is 40? Just what *is* intelligence in an adult? But the twentieth century adores rating things, and so IQ scores came to be regarded as a measure of actual intelligence rather than academic aptitude. The test score became king. (Roger Peters mischievously suggests that this may be why the people who take tests are called "subjects.")

One disgruntled researcher even came up with a satire of IQ tests, which was printed in the *American Journal of Sociology.* The Cn Test, devised by F. Adler in 1947, measures C.

Adler's Cn Test

1. How many hours did you sleep last night? _____

2. Estimate the length of your nose in inches and multiply by 2. _____

3. Do you like fried liver? (Mark 1 for Yes, —2 for No.) _____

4. How many feet are there in a yard? _____

5. Estimate the number of glasses of ginger ale the inventor of this test drank while inventing it. _____

Add the above items. The sum is your crude Cn-score. This test is to be taken daily at the same hour of the day for as long as you can take it.

And what is C? "C," Adler responded, "is what the tests measure."

THE VALUE OF MISTAKES

One benefit of the formalized IQ tests is that the "wrong" answers are frequently as interesting as the "right" ones. Dr. Howard Gardner writes about Swiss psychologist Jean Piaget, who was intrigued by the "mistakes" that children make when taking IQ tests. For example, if you show a hammer to four-year-olds and ask them to find something similar in a group of objects, most will choose a nail instead of a screwdriver. They reason that hammers pound nails (interaction), instead of grouping hammers and screwdrivers under the common category of tools. Similarly they are more likely to match "milk" to "glass" than to "water," and "fingers" to "hand" rather than "toes." Piaget based his highly regarded theories of human intellectual growth on his studies of the reasoning behind these errors.

IQ AND SUCCESS

Does having a high IQ test score mean you are going to be more successful? The answer is an unequivocal "yes and no." Probably "yes," because some of the skills that go into good academic work —working in groups under a leader; performing tasks competently, completely, and on time; showing up day after day, year after year—are highly regarded in the workplace. And possibly "no," because if you think trying to get a definition of "intelligence" is hard, try getting any agreement on what constitutes "success"! Even in our materialistic times, reports Daniel Yankelovich in his book *New Rules,* the majority of people questioned in one poll defined "success" as self-realization instead of status or income. Obviously pleasure with one's life is not based on an IQ score.

Even if we accept that many people mean "productivity, prestige, and better-than-average income" when they say "success," then IQ test scores are only one small factor. Various studies indicate that the correlation between IQ score and income is about .5. That is, 50 percent of the people studied have IQ scores and incomes that both fall in the same category: high, medium, or low. This also means that 50 percent have unrelated IQ scores and income levels. The correlation between IQ and social status is also about .5 or 50 percent. When you get to job performance, as rated by supervisors and coworkers, the percentage starts at 50 percent and drops as low as 20 percent! Whatever your definition of success, there are obviously many contributing factors besides academic aptitude.

IQ scores reveal nothing about other human attributes like creativity, adaptability, and sociability, or about managerial skills such as innovation, delegation, negotiation, discretion, sensitivity, and skepticism. Cognitive psychologist Roger Peters believes that the IQ test "reveals little about an individual's potential for further growth." Two people may have similar scores and seem to be cruising along at the same speed, yet one is already going at top speed, while the other is still in first gear. (Aesop had a less contemporary metaphor for potential versus performance. He called it the fable of *The Tortoise and the Hare.*)

There *are* some advantages to having high test scores. One is known as the Pygmalion effect. According to *Pygmalion in the Classroom* by Robert Rosenthal and Lenore Jacobson, when a child scores well on a test, teachers and parents develop expectations that can become a self-fulfilling prophecy. In one experiment, teachers were told that randomly selected children had shown exceptional promise on special tests. At the end of the school year, all those children showed marked improvement in their class work and grades, although the teachers believed that they had not shown the students any favoritism. We *all* respond in some way to others' expectations, positive or negative. Even when we resolve not to be influenced by an IQ test score, Ray and Myers in their *Creativity in Business* remind us of Werner K. Heisenberg's Uncertainty Principle which states that "the mere act of observing something changes the nature of the thing observed."

HOW MANY KINDS OF INTELLIGENCE?

One. By the late 1920s, English researcher Charles Spearman decided that intelligence had become "a word with so many meanings that finally it had none." In *The Abilities of Man* he theorized that we each possess just one general capacity which he called *g*, and that this capacity to "[discover] relations and correlates" can be applied in all areas of life.

Three. The ancient Greeks and Romans divided the mind's operations into three areas: reason, will, and feeling.

Seven. L. L. Thurston, a researcher who worked with Thomas Edison, felt seven was a more accurate number. He suggested that we have seven Primary Mental Abilities (PMA): spatial visualization, perceptual ability, verbal comprehension, numerical ability, memory, word fluency, and reasoning.

Thirty-Seven. Eighteenth century physician Franz Joseph Gall, creator of phrenology, came up with a list of 37 powers of the mind. For many years, people enjoyed judging the intellect and disposition of others, using Gall's system of measuring bumps on the head.

There were even learned treatises on identifying criminal types by their skulls. Gall's attempts to analyze the brain's interior by its external shape are no longer taken seriously, but he *was* one of the first to suggest that different parts of the brain control different functions. Another of his theories is enjoying new study: Gall argued that rather than having one set of general mental powers such as perception, memory, and attention, we have a separate set of these powers for each of our abilities—language, music, vision, etc.

One Hundred Fifty. Stanford psychologist Joy Paul Guilford proposes that we actually have 150 different and separate intelligences. Her list of "vectors" consists of five kinds of operations, five kinds of contents, and six kinds of products ($5 \times 5 = 25 \times 6 = 150$). To compute a person's intelligence accurately, according to Guilford, it would be necessary to test all 150 areas.

STYLES OF INTELLIGENCE

Do bright, productive people work differently from others? A familiar model of intelligence used productively is the high-powered executive. Psychometrician Norman Fredericksen devised a test to evaluate business people. He had his subjects go through an "in basket" of fictional memos, letters, contracts, files, and phone call slips, then did a complex statistical analysis of how each person approached and responded to this tangle of information. Fredericksen concluded that "people who prepare for actions, who have high work outputs, and who frequently seek help tend to be more successful than people who act impulsively, slowly, and alone."

An even more complex test of executive responses was done by three cognitive psychologists from Penn State's College of Medicine and from Princeton University, as described by Siegfreid Steufert, et al., in *Human Information Processing*. Their subjects were presented with a simulated fast-developing business crisis and bombarded with relevant and irrelevant business information by phone, computer, and VCR while they were hooked up to stress indicators that measured things like heartbeat. The psychologists concluded that style— "cognitive complexity"—rather than IQ produced the best results. They described cognitive complexity as the ability to handle many different kinds of information from many different sources without getting overloaded. Can you stop one task and start another without missing a beat? Many top executives possess this skill, but it is also common among people who work under pressure with both people and things: chefs, fire fighters, medical workers, teachers, film directors, generals, and parents.

Two people, equally smart, can think very differently. This is called one's "thinking style" or "cognitive style." Practical intelligence, according to psychologists and management consultants, emphasizes qualities like skepticism, a bias for action, cognitive complexity, intuition, and creativity. Your cognitive style is *how* you think, not how *well* you think. There may be some relation between cognitive style and the particular skill or intelligence to which it is being applied. Here is how psychologist Nathan Kogan illustrates this theory in *Moderators of Competence*.

	Left Brain	**Right Brain**
Multiple intelligences	verbal logical	spatial body
Cognitive styles	analytic methodical reflective	holistic intuitive active

Harvard psychologist Howard Gardner's theory of Multiple Intelligences divides the mind's abilities differently:

- Linguistic/Verbal

- Musical—pitch and rhythm (separate from linguistic intelligence except in languages based on pitch changes, such as Chinese)

- Logical/Mathematical

- Spatial

- Bodily—coordination and dexterity

- Interpersonal—awareness of and sensitivity to others

- Intrapersonal—self-knowledge

Obviously individual abilities in each of these areas can vary greatly. Psychologist Roger Peters notes that people with Down's syndrome often have low levels of linguistic and logical intelligence and of sense of self, but high levels of social intelligence—they are good at dealing with people. Also, says Peters, people with right-brain injuries often keep their verbal abilities, but become socially out of sync. Dr. Howard Gardner reports that some Alzheimer's victims lose spatial, linguistic, and logical skills but keep their social sensitivity.

Cognitive styles are undergoing a lot of study, but there doesn't seem to be any particular relation between style and intelligence. They occur in every possible combination.

SEXUAL EQUALITY OF THE BRAIN

No sooner had definite skills been assigned to the left and right hemispheres of the brain than some early studies indicated that men's and women's brains worked differently. More recent research indicates that these early findings were based on inadequate or misinterpreted data. Internationally known neuropsychologist Marcel Kinsbourne experimented to find out which side of the brain men and women use most. Tests in which people balanced a pencil on a finger (visuospatial task) while speaking (verbal task) and eye tests—which way you roll your eyes when you consider verbal or visuospatial tests—indicated that male and female brains behave similarly.

Another early experiment at Columbia University indicated that females had more connecting fiber between their brains, that they were more "symmetrical" because their brain halves could talk to each other. But this study involved only nine males and five females! A 1986 University of Wisconsin study of 39 men and women showed no differences.

Boys and girls perform differently on some tests, with boys excelling at spatial tests such as mazes—*the first time.* Paula Caplan, a researcher at the Institute for Studies in Education at Toronto, discovered that this advantage disappears when the test is given a second time to the same group. Caplan suggests that boys may already be familiar with these spatial tasks because of cultural encouragement. Caplan says, "Some scientists have claimed in all seriousness that this [advantage] is because the so-called female hormones make us dumb and the so-called male hormones make them smart. This is the kind of claim that can be . . . accepted and get into the newspapers and textbooks and cocktail party conversation, where it's now assumed that males are better at math than females because of that hormonal difference. This is very primitive thinking."

LEARNING TO BE SMARTER

As we have already seen, people can learn to be intelligent. Many of the systems for organizing information, primarily language, must be learned. School can make you smarter, although not always in the ways that educators imagine. Researchers J. Goody et al. reported in Africa on several years spent studying literacy patterns among a group of Vai in Liberia. Some were literate only in English, some only in Arabic, and about 20 percent of the adult males had learned a special Vai syllabary script devised in the nineteenth century for letter writing and record keeping.

The researchers concluded that even a high degree of literacy in any of the languages was far less important to general thinking ability than the *process* by which that literacy was obtained: attending school. The activities in the school situation were more responsible for developing problem solving, classification, and analytic skills, and even sensitivity to language, than anything learned by reading alone. But don't write off studying, in or out of school. We learn to learn. "When knowledge is processed correctly," says Roger Peters, "it makes room for new knowledge. . . ."

INTELLIGENCE AND ADVANCING AGE

Until recently, "old age" and "senility" were considered synonymous. Now we know that loss of intellect as we grow older is caused by identifiable medical and psychological problems that include Alzheimer's Disease, cardiovascular disease (or the lifestyle that brings it on), reactions to medication, poor nutrition, depression, and isolation. If we're moderately healthy, we don't run out of brain cells, but we may let them get weak and flabby through lack of use.

As infants, we produce a lot more neuronal fibers than we will ever need. Writing in *Nature*, Jean-Pierre Changeux and Antoine Danchin tell us these provide a safety margin, so that we can survive a lot of bumps on the head without affecting our intelligence. When a child takes one of the inevitable tumbles, the brain cells go into high gear, producing as much as six weeks' worth of growth in the next 72 hours. After our neurons have formed into synaptic connections (the electrical circuits of the brain), the excess 15 percent to 85 percent of the neurons are discarded. We have so many that some infants have literally lost half their brains to illness or injury and still developed normally. The extra neurons hang around and take up the slack. But a few years later when the circuits have all "set," a head injury can result in permanent impairment.

Those essential synaptic connections are locked in the brain by intellectual and sensual stimulation. Unless we use them, they are discarded. Cats who never see certain line formations in their first months of life lose their ability to see them as adults. Similarly infants deprived of intellectual and sensual stimulation will fail to develop mentally and may even die, although all their physical needs are met.

A somewhat similar situation occurs when we get older. Older people who are functioning at a high level of ability constantly seek out stimulating situations. But which is the cause and which the effect? Certainly high ability can *cause* the search for stimulation. But would the reverse be true? Can providing a stimulating environment slow down, prevent, or even *reverse* mental decline?

A thirty-year study by researchers at Pennsylvania State University, reported in *Developmental Psychology*, showed that very few people experience any decline in their intellectual abilities before their 60s. From then on, the number of people experiencing age-related decline increases markedly for every seven-year interval. However, many are unimpaired in their 70s and some are still in top form in their 80s.

To find out whether intellectual decline can be halted or reversed, researchers K. Warner Schaie and Sherry L. Willis studied 229 members of the same group health organization, aged 64 to 95 years. Slightly more than half the group had lost some mental ability during the previous 14 years and the others had not. The subjects each agreed to take five hours of special training in either reasoning or spatial skills. Both the "decliners" and the "stables" showed an increase in ability. Those who had been declining showed a 55 percent increase in spatial ability and 60 percent increase in reasoning. Those who had remained stable during the 14 years since they were first tested now showed a 39 percent increase in spatial ability and a 53.6 percent improvement in reasoning skills.

The researchers speculated that they had succeeded in "reactivat[ing] behaviors and skills that have remained in the subjects' behavioral repertory but that have not been actively employed." The degree of improvement was unrelated to the age, education, or income of subjects. The researchers proved that it is possible for older people to reverse decline or enhance performance in these two intellectual abilities.

BRAIN AEROBICS

No matter what our age, we all need mental stimulation to keep us flexible and healthy. (The fact that you're reading this book shows that you're already keeping your mind in good shape.) Try some of the following exercises.

Increase your circle of acquaintances. Traveling through life is like running a marathon: many start, but the ranks thin out toward the finish line. Start now to cultivate lots of younger *and* older acquaintances. It will make you more flexible and you'll be surprised how many acquaintances will become friends.

Your assignment:

• Approach three people who are at least 15 years younger or older than yourself and say something sincere that will stimulate them to feel especially good about themselves. No strings attached. Don't push. Repeat at least once a week.

• Choose the most "difficult" person you know and see if you can exchange at least three sentences without getting in an argument or taking a defensive position. Make a game of diverting the conversation to neutral ground whenever the person complains, attacks, or makes an outrageous statement. Repeat once a week.

• Do the same with someone whose beliefs are profoundly different from yours. Keep trying until you find a common ground of interest.

Think ahead. Most of us have a short attention span—a few days or months. If you doubt that, try recalling what was the most important issue in your life last month. Last year? Ten years ago? Business and political leaders are usually comfortable planning way beyond their lifetime.

In *Quilts and Women's Lives,* filmmaker Pat Ferrero interviewed two sisters who, at ages 74 and 76, started a ten-year plan to make quilts for their 17 nieces and nephews. They began by cutting out the pieces for all 17 quilts, then finished them one by one. "How many of us," commented Ms. Ferrero, "have a ten-year plan at age 24 or 34 or 54?" Of course these two remarkable sisters completed their 17 quilts.

Your assignment:

• Jot down an outline of your intended activities for the next year.

• Jot down a five-year plan.

• Write a paragraph describing yourself in 20 years.

• Buy a five-year date book and use it. (Certain executives and all opera stars can't live without them!)

Stretch. Patterns are comforting and essential for productivity in many activities. When they don't exist, humans tend to create them. Yet, stepping out of the pattern occasionally gives us a valuable jolt of new perspective.

Your assignment (do one of the following):

• Take a different route when you go to the store or office. What do you notice?

• Eat a meal in an entirely different place than you usually eat. Is the meal less satisfying? More?

• Read one chapter of a book that you would never be caught dead reading—a frivolous romance, a gritty western, a civics textbook. Is your original prejudice reconfirmed?

• Ask someone to show you how to do something. Really listen to what they say and then do it their way.

• Sit in a public place. Make five predictions about what the people around you will do: "That man is going to stand up soon." "The next person through that door will be a woman." When you get three out of five right, quit.

Play. Keep your middle-of-the-brain limbic tissues toned up by living in the *now.* Excite your wondering mind.

Your assignment:

• Once a day, play a game: checkers, chess, bridge, tennis, polo, pick-up-sticks. Total involvement and enthusiasm is essential. Winning (or even finishing) is optional.

• When you're alone, put on some music and dance. Pretend you're Ginger Rogers, Michael Jackson, Nijinsky. No one is looking. If you're in a full body cast, drum your fingers, roll your eyes, wiggle your ears in time to the music.

• Find a book that you enjoyed as a child and reread it.

• Give a spur-of-the-moment party.

• Work a jigsaw puzzle.

• Get down on the floor to play marbles or jacks. Give yourself ten extra points for jumping rope or playing hopscotch.

• Draw a picture of the most dignified person you know. Show this person doing something silly. (Don't let anyone see it, if it might offend someone.)

• Go to a parade or circus and cheer your head off.

Learn. Stimulate the cortex. Keep yourself supplied with new experiences.
Your assignment:

• Stay on top of an important international news story. Memorize the names of all the key figures. Research the background issues at the library. Engage your friends with your expertise.

• Design and make something you've never made before: a dog house, an afghan, chili, a back scratcher. Here process is much more important than product.

• Read at least three different books about a single famous person. Do the authors disagree on facts or motivations? What do *you* think?

• Plan something important: an investment strategy, a garden, a major home alteration, a trip around the world. How do you gather information? Get advice? Make the final decisions?

• Study something new: piano, tap dancing, Turkish, tax preparation, medieval art.

• Go for a walk. Don't laugh—a University of Utah study showed that a brisk walk three times a week improves elderly people's mental alertness and memory. Dr. Robert Dustman, professor of neurology and psychology at the University, speculated that the increased oxygen capacity from such exercise can maintain and even restore mental ability. The report in *Neurobiology of Aging* traced 43 sedentary volunteers, aged 55 to 70, who were divided into three groups. One group remained sedentary. One did regular stretching exercises. The third did a full-scale, gradually increasing program of aerobic conditioning. The surprise was that the stretching group also showed a modest gain. "I suppose those people were so out of shape that even stretching was an improvement," Dustman commented.

13

HOW TO
CHANGE YOUR MIND:
USING CUES AND
CONVERSATIONS

Until now, you probably thought your behavior and feelings were cued by what was happening around you. You couldn't *help* feeling mad or sad or bad, confused or overwhelmed.

But by now I hope you have begun to realize that the various parts of your mind discuss each outside event and decide on your response. That response is based in different ratios on your personal needs and the needs and expectations of those around you. One part of your mind notices an occurrence. Another assesses how society expects you to respond and how you have actually responded in the past. You may supply an emotion. Your mental executive approves or disapproves of your total reaction, considering your personal needs and the requirements of society.

That amorphous entity, "society," provides lots of cues and requirements for our responses. Society is made up of all humanity, descending in tighter and tighter circles to the humans in our most intimate circle. Culture, religion, political beliefs, philosophy, custom, geography, language, temperament—all provide cues that we respond to more or less automatically. The automatic part saves us thousands of decisions every day and makes life simpler and easier. But when the automatic part blinds us to better options, we need to discover that we have choices. We can choose a different response.

WHAT IS A CUE?

Nothing represents a "cue" better than a flag. It is an entirely abstract symbol that can be responded to with almost any emotion. Run a flag up the flagpole and the viewer can feel:

- Pride and patriotism

- Joy because it represents victory

- Sorrow or fear because it represents defeat

- Anger because it represents oppression

- Embarrassment because it represents subjugation

- Excitement—"Cheer them!"

- Blood lust—"Kill them!"

- Boredom because another political speech is imminent

Funerals are another example of a cue to both emotions and behavior. Sorrow for the living and joy for the departed are displayed in various ratios in different cultures. Some cultures hold parties with laughter and feasting to celebrate the departed's journey to a better place. Others require the survivors to withdraw from the pleasures of life. Some cultures, like contemporary China, practice total stoicism in the face of death. Others expect violent expressions of grief. Tribal women in Papua New Guinea cut off a finger as a sign of mourning; some older women have no fingers at all. In India, despite vigorous government efforts, there are still isolated cases of *suttee*, ritual suicide by a wife following the death of her husband. Because America embraces so many cultures, a wide variety of responses to death are acceptable (short of *suttee*.) This tolerance is admirable, but it can also be confusing. We may not be sure what is expected of us. However we respond, someone is bound to write to Dear Abby complaining about our actions. The fewer options permitted by a society, the less chance of unintentionally offending public sensibilities. (Interestingly, *any* ritual for the dead helps the survivors grieve and begin the healing process.)

ASSOCIATING CUES AND FEELINGS

How do you know when to be happy? Angry? What cues do you give yourself? Could you change your response to a specific cue? Could you give yourself predetermined cues when you want to feel a certain way, just as actors cue themselves to cry or laugh?

Remember the list of emotions in chapter 11 and the situations that usually cued you to experience them? This is the beginning of your cue list. Let's say that a particular song usually makes you sad. Do you want to change that cue or use it? Thinking about that song may be a valuable way for you to get in touch with your feelings when you want to mourn or work through depression. However, if that song is played several times a day by the Muzak where you work and tears are inappropriate, you may wish to change your response to it. You have the choice of keeping or discarding the connection between this cue and your response.

Some associations are more ingrained. Anger at injustice, sorrow over loss, happiness over good fortune are fairly basic and entirely appropriate. But you probably would like to avoid auto-cues that "make" you afraid, sad, angry when you would prefer to feel another way. You can also cue yourself to be happy, content, calm, even loving.

Now is the time to go over the lists you made on pages 181 and 182. You were asked to list things that you usually respond to in different ways: happiness, sadness, anger, fear, excitement, contentment/calm, love. Then you were asked to go back over your list and mark any of your responses that you wanted to change. You may have written an alternate response to the occasion in the margin.

WHAT MAKES A CUE?

Your life is full of cues right now. Some are used by others to manipulate you. You use others consciously to help yourself. Some typical cues are special clothing, music, smells, tastes, verbal patterns, key words and phrases, body positions, colors, textures, environments, physical activities. Some classic sets of cues are:

- Loud band music playing a Sousa march, uniforms, flags, marching people, prancing horses, the smell of fireworks, the flash of brass buttons.

- Loud band music playing circus melodies, brightly colored costumes, flags, marching people, prancing horses, the smell of popcorn and cotton candy, the flash of sequins.

- Loud band music playing a funeral dirge, brightly colored flowers, flags at half staff, marching people, prancing horses, the smell of gunpowder as cannons fire a salute, the flash of the sun on military sabers held in salute.

Your response to a military parade, a circus parade, and a state funeral might be similar in many ways, but you would be unlikely to feel patriotic at a circus or hilarity and childlike wonder at a funeral. How about your feelings with these cues:

> Loud band music playing "The Stripper," brightly colored costumes, prancing chorus girls, the smell of whiskey and sweat and stale cigarette smoke, the flash of sequins, the feeling of a sticky floor beneath your feet.

What feelings are cued? Patriotism? Somber grief? Probably not. Your responses are partly cultural, partly personal. You might choose to feel anger, anxiety, or disgust rather than the more common responses to any of these sets of cues.

REWRITING CUES

When a cue has outlived its usefulness, you can decide to change it. Or you can look for a cue in a difficult situation that lets you respond the way you want to. First, here are some examples of changing outmoded cues.

> As soon as I walk in the door at work, I start bristling. This man in my department, Charlie, he knows just

how to needle me, how to get my goat. Even though I
know I shouldn't 'bite', I end up shouting and
humiliated while he just sits there grinning.

Does Charlie attack you in any special way? Or is it his manner? If he attacks you about one particular thing, use cues to
desensitize yourself about that issue. If he always picks on your
physical appearance, ancestry, or beliefs, make mental notes of the
phrases he uses and turn them around. "Big nose"—picture your
magnificent nose as dozens of admirers point at it in wonder and awe.
Hear their voices raised in praise. Envision all the great noses of
history, from Louis XIV to Barbra Streisand. As the adulation grows
louder, hear Charlie's voice join them. You smile, happy that he has
at long last recognized your magnificent nose.

"You fat slob . . ." Do the same with images of illustrious girth,
commanding corpulence, peerless, prominent poundage. Summon
up role models—kings and queens, emperors and divas. Again, let
Charlie join the chorus of praise as you smile condescendingly. Use
similar strategies for racial, religious, political slurs. If he calls you
something that you definitely are not—"pinko fascist" or "chauvinist
pig"—summon images of illustrious people of history who were
called ridiculous names by their opponents. (Galileo, Pasteur,
Columbus, Eleanor Roosevelt, and Gandhi can start your list.) Don't
take the posture of a martyr. Just step into the skin of your role
model, never faltering in your contentment and self-assurance as
these absurdities roll off you and bounce across the floor.

Maybe it's not what Charlie says but his insulting manner that
makes you see red. Again, pick a cue from his appearance, voice,
expressions, or even the setting in which he delivers his comments.
Maybe he comes up to you in the cafeteria where there are smells of
food, formica tables, plastic plants. Consider any or all of these cues
as potential triggers for benevolent or warm, safe feelings. In what
situation do you feel parental, in control? What cues currently
signal that response? How can you use the cues of the cafeteria to
help you recreate that feeling? Perhaps you feel in control when you
are supervising small children. The stainless steel of the cafeteria
could suggest a high chair tray. Food smells provide lots of cues for
recalling safe, contented times. Or maybe you feel calm and col-
lected when you are in a library, a church, the lobby of a posh hotel.

Not easy to find similar cues in a bustling cafeteria, but they are there: Books with their unique feel and smell can be carried in; the wood of a chair or light coming through a window can suggest a chapel; the buff walls can become marble in your imaginary hotel lobby. Practice cueing your contented feelings with similar cues in other places or in the cafeteria when Charlie isn't around.

Cues can be internal also. To combat Charlie's control cues over you, remember an exciting or interesting time when you called the shots. Use psychologist Richard Bandler's "swishing" technique. Reexperience the pleasurable sensation. Then imagine Charlie's face. Dwell on it for a few moments, then quickly return to the pleasurable in-control image. Switch back and forth a few more times. Now slowly make your mental picture of Charlie black and white while keeping the pleasurable image in full color. Switch images again. When you return to Charlie's taunting face, you can maintain the pleasurable feelings. Charlie may sneer, leer, smirk, but he has no power over your feelings. He is ineffective. Ineffectual. Simply spinning his wheels. Silly Charlie. The old cue was Charlie. The old response was anger, embarrassment, loss of control. The new cue is still Charlie. The new response is calm, contentment, control, a feeling of inner strength.

> My mother died last year and I still miss her a lot. Anything that reminds me of her makes me sad and depressed.

You are using the cue "mother" to summon images of how much you have lost. Fortunately, you probably have lots of happy, uplifting memories about your times together. Make a list of the cues that stimulate sadness. Then concentrate on reversing the cues by summoning new images. The smell of a pot roast? Any funny story you have about one of your mother's pot roasts? A particular song? Any happy event this song recalls for you? Play the song in your head as you focus on this past moment. If you feel very down at first, keep repeating the song until you've exhausted the sad images and get to the warm, fulfilling ones. Periodically replay the song and experience the uplift of positive thoughts about your mother.

Is there something you always did together, something she did for you, some place you went together? Are these things and places painful now? Put yourself physically or mentally in one of these situations. Experience the pain. This situation will never again be quite the same. What was good about it? Reexperience the pleasure, the fun. Then try to go back and feel bad again. Now reexperience the good stuff again. Do you have a choice now?

Maybe your mother had a special way of looking at you, something special she said or did for you. Again, recreate the moment in your mind. This will never happen again, except in your imagination. If these images invite misery, you can choose not to experience them again. However, if they make you feel loved and cared for, you can have them again any time you want. You have a choice.

I hate bugs.

Phobias can be highly complex or simply a response to what others expect of you. Notice that you said "hate," not "fear." Lots of children, especially girls, learn that making a fuss about bugs, snakes, mice, even dogs and cats, can win them attention and protection. Why give up the glorious drama? As an adult you will probably try to surround yourself with people who will support your self-image. What's the use of fainting over a water beetle if no one is going to notice?

But maybe the energy this posture requires is needed elsewhere. Never going anywhere that might have bugs, mice, etc., has become restricting. But—surprise—you really do feel a sharp tummy twinge when you spot a spider or a spaniel. You have created a cue that you no longer ignore.

Time to re-cue. Sit in a quiet place and imagine a square on a distant wall. It is a very tiny black and white photograph. You can't quite make out what it is a picture of. You order the picture to advance toward you so you can see it better. It slides toward you until you recognize it is a bug. You order the picture to recede. Now you're sitting there and you're getting kind of bored. Why not slide the picture forward again and see what happens? Remember, you are in control and can move the picture in any direction at any speed you want. It is still only a photograph.

When you are comfortable with this black and white photo, replace it with a movie, still in black and white. In this movie you walk into a room and see the picture of the bug on the wall. If this is too uncomfortable, reverse the film and watch yourself walk out of the room backwards. When you are comfortable with the movie of yourself walking up to the picture of the bug, step inside the movie and experience yourself walking up to the picture. Do this until it is comfortable. Then step out of the movie and watch yourself walk up to a real, live bug. When this is comfortable, step into the film and experience yourself walking up to the bug. Say, "Hi, bug. I'm bigger than you are and smarter. I can swat you or scoop you up and toss you out the door." (This is only if the feared object is really harmless. If it is potentially lethal, maintaining a healthy respect—not *fear*—is the sign of a prudent person.)

Finally, try it all in color. Go back and repeat any stage if the new one becomes too uncomfortable.

Here are some examples of selecting cues in difficult situations that can help you respond the way you want to.

> My mother-in-law is always critical of me. She smiles
> and says very polite things, but I can see that her lips
> are tight and she is always giving a little sniff. I
> tighten up and no one has much fun. I dread being
> with her.

Whether or not your mother-in-law is really critical, or you are just interpreting her sinus condition as disapproval, you can use her behavior to cue new responses. While it would be easy to use her mannerisms to trigger disparaging images of her as weak or inferior, you decide that in the long run you would do better to like her. Start with that sniff. Did anyone you really like ever sniff? Is there anything pleasant that makes a sniffing sound? A cute, pink-nosed rabbit, a favorite puppy, a lovable film or television personality? Or maybe the sound is similar to the soft rasp of a wood plane as you work with sweet-smelling wood, or the rush of water past your ears as you swim, or the rustle of real silk against your skin. Find a positive image for the sound. Then imagine your mother-in-law sniffing. Hold the image for a few seconds, then quickly imagine the positive sound. Experience the warm glow. Then switch to mother-in-law. Switch back and forth over and over until you can stop on mother-in-law and still experience the warm feelings. Now clear your mind and then experience your mother-in-law. The warm flow should return. If not, repeat the process.

Continue doing this with anything else about her that can provide a cue. It could be her perfume, the kind of clothes she usually wears, her hairstyle, the sound of her voice, her speech mannerisms, the place where you usually see her. In each case, match her cue with an outside cue that is usually an occasion for you to feel comfortable, contented, friendly, loving, warm, open.

> I've just moved to a new community and everything
> feels very strange and unfriendly. I want to make new
> friends, but I'm shy and don't know where to start.

First, decide how you want to feel when you approach new people and situations. Curious? Confident? Happy? Go back to the list of personal cues you started in chapter 11, pages 181 and 182, and find experiences that may trigger these feelings. Most of us already have routines and talismans that help us feel confident and happy. It may be clothes that we know make us look good, having a new haircut, the "right" car or jewelry or credit card. But all these may not be enough when we find ourselves in an entirely new situation.

Start by finding new cues that hook you into the old feelings you want to recreate. Be alert to everything new and exciting. Look for parallels and similarities as well as differences. Part of you is still mourning your old home. You can withdraw or you can notice what's new.

But noticing alone won't ingratiate you with your new neighbors and coworkers. You want to project the "real" you as accurately as possible, without nervousness, false heartiness, or protective aloofness. When you meet someone new, try picking a friendly face from the past that this person reminds you of. Temporarily, cue your behavior and responses to your old friend's image superimposed over this new person. His reactions will quickly help you adjust to his reality.

Perhaps you have to cope with new objects. You never in your life have encountered an electric stove, a push-button telephone, a gearshift car, and an oil furnace. Meeting them all at once can be overwhelming. Try relating each to some mechanical device that you feel confident about. Instead of approaching them with despair, cue yourself with the confidence you felt holding a test tube over a Bunsen burner in chemistry class, the excitement of poking out the holes on a Lotto card, or the thrill you felt when you worked the tractor gearshift that summer on the farm as a kid.

Maybe the outdoors looks very different. Hills where you are used to flatland. Or wet when you are used to dry. Go back to similar images in heartwarming movies, books, TV shows. When you step out your door and everything looks very strange, even a bit hostile, cue yourself to the pleasure this image has given you in the past in your mind. Use the air, sun, temperature, wind to cue pleasant associations. Imagine that your favorite local hero or heroine is about to walk into view. This land is their land, this land is *your* land now.

> My father is always criticizing me about my job and
> how I handle money. He makes me feel like I'm five
> years old every time he starts in on me. Then I
> wonder if I really know what I'm doing.

Redecision psychotherapist Mary Goulding has a "ventriloquist" technique for this kind of nagging, whether the voice is from someone else or our own minds. First, make the statement formally:

> You don't handle your money properly.

> You'll never succeed.

> You'll end up broke and in the gutter.

Then imagine someone really ridiculous—a witch, a grotesque clown—who is repeating these words over and over. Make the figure pretty silly and repulsive. You can even imagine drool coming from its mouth as it says these things about you. As you listen, the voice becomes more and more ludicrous, higher pitched, singsong, whiny. Soon the words blur and become a stream of sounds like the childhood nyeh-nyeh-nyeh. How do you respond to the message now? Are you still strongly affected by it? Or has it lost its ability to disturb and disrupt you?

DIFFERENT RESPONSES TO SIMILAR EVENTS

Two famous opera singers show how differently two people can respond to a similar event. One had a magnificent mother, the other a magnificent husband. When the magnificent husband died, the famous German soprano left the stage and retired at the height of her career. She had sung chiefly to give him pleasure and now had no more need to perform. Her life was full and happy offstage and out of the spotlight.

The child of the magnificent mother had a different experience. Unlike many stage mothers, this mother was adored by all, a prime force behind her daughter's career. "Without Mama, I'd never have sung a note," she admitted. Then Mama died. The singer was desolate and stopped singing. Many assumed that, since Mama was gone, the singer's career was over. But a curious thing happened. The singer, always stout and homely, began to lose weight, take an interest in clothes and hairstyles, attend parties where she was no longer in the shadow of her beloved mother. She literally blossomed; her singing (always splendid) actually improved. She become a breathtaking and desirable woman as well as a star.

Both these prima donnas responded similarly to their initial loss. But then their Organizing Minds went to work, evaluating how much satisfaction each of their Reacting Minds gained from their individual singing careers. Finally their Executive Minds decided whether or not to resume singing. The answers, obviously, were very different, but right for each of them.

TALKING TO YOURSELF

When you talk to yourself, does one part of your mind hog the floor? Is another part constantly being told to shut up? Each part of the mind has a special thing that it does very well. The job of the mental executive is to make sure everyone makes a contribution to the conversation and to solicit opinions from the appropriate part of the mind when something specific comes along. This can be quite a job if one part of the mind is naturally bossy or just highly developed.

Jerry was faced with an unfortunately common problem. His elderly mother, Mabel, could no longer care for herself. She was living all alone in the large house that had been her home for 50 years. The mortgage had long since been paid off and the yearly taxes were nominal. All Mabel's children had been born there and some of her grandchildren.

Jerry analyzed the situation, weighing the different options. One of Mabel's five children could move into the home and care for her, but they each lived in different cities and had families and careers of their own. A live-in nurse or a day-nurse could be hired, but this person would be hard to supervise long-distance. Mabel could go to live with one of her children, but this would also be difficult. Or Mabel could go to a nursing home.

Jerry's organizing ability was highly developed and usually got the rest of his mind to agree. The most efficient thing, he decided, would be to sell the house and use the money to put his mother in a nursing home. This was a logical decision, possibly the only decision. However, it was made without the contributions of Jerry's emotions and senses: that his mother felt that her home was part of her and she was part of her home. A switch to an impersonal nursing home, even a good one, would mean a crippling loss of identity for a proud and independent woman.

Obviously, any important decision needs to be framed by the analytical part of the mind, but a common mistake is to ignore equally valid input from the other non-analytical minds. Without democratic input from the entire mind, rebellion is a possibility. Only when you have looked at an issue with each part of your mind can a difficult and painful decision be made without future guilt or recriminations.

Another person in Jerry's position might be overwhelmed by opposing messages between dispassionate analysis and emotion, and opt for an emotionally satisfying but illogical solution, like sacrificing his career to care for his mother, or abandoning his mother entirely, or even, in a state of total mental conflict, considering killing his mother to end "her" (actually his) suffering. This would be an extreme case, but it demonstrates what can happen when the reacting and organizing parts of the mind short circuit each other and block solutions from the problem-solving imagination.

The one factor that Jerry wasn't including in his mental conversations was his creativity. Were there any other options? Mabel had many good friends in the area. Perhaps one of them, younger and abler, was now widowed and in tight financial circumstances. If so, perhaps this friend would consider moving into Mabel's large house as a companion for Mabel and as supervisor of a reliable part-time housekeeper/cook. This would be considerably cheaper and keep Mabel in her home. Maybe one of Mabel's grandchildren would consider attending the local college and living with Mabel, in order to supervise a day-nurse. Or maybe Mabel herself might have some suggestions to offer. By getting every part of his mind involved in a conversation, Jerry was much more likely to come up with a creative solution.

CONFERENCES AND CONVERSATIONS

Most of the time you really won't be listening to your own mental conversations. As long as things go smoothly, you take this background babble for granted. But when you slow down or feel stymied, then your mental executive has the option of polling the delegation to see what is happening. You have already explored the different interests and talents of each part of your mind. It is up to you to make use of their skills, just like a good chairman at a board meeting.

Studies of the group process among people, as reported in *MIS* quarterly, show that groups with mixed cognitive styles are more effective than groups where everyone "speaks the same language." When group members have a variety of viewpoints, they are more likely to see the flaws in each other's approaches. The conclusion: include people of different cognitive styles on committees and decision-making teams. Fortunately for the committee of your mind, your perfect team is already assembled. You already have experts on everything the mind is capable of doing and perceiving.

A typical conference of the minds runs like this:

Steps	Key Speaker(s)	What Speakers Do
Decision to hold conference	Mental executive	States purpose of get-together, what needs to be resolved. Supervises input by entire mind during Phases 1 and 2 below.
Phase 1—Goal and mission setting or identifying areas of concern	Wondering and Reacting minds	Imagine, troubleshoot, fantasize, project, use intuitive thinking, look at all aspects of the situation, try playful approach to problems and solutions, explore feelings about all facets, seek broadest overview possible, seek perspective on all considerations.
Phase 2— Planning and evaluation	Organizing mind	Organizes plan, resolves details, fine-tunes, points out logistical problems.
Resolution	Mental executive	Decides on course of action, enlists entire mind to carry it out.

Like a good manager, you need to identify the right part of your mind for the job and then persuade it to do its best. When coordination is necessary, your mental executive combats arguments and apathy with pleas, coercion, the psychology of a star salesman, and the charms of a Circe.

USING ODORS AS CUES

I use this exercise when I teach people how to break through writing blocks. I have 50 small vials with substances in them: vinegar, cinnamon, pine oil, lavender, oil of roses, peppermint, turpentine, detergent, etc. Each workshop participant chooses a vial at random, sniffs it, then, eyes closed, lets the impressions rush up. You can do this too, but in reverse.

Shut your eyes and imagine a situation in which you are comfortable, happy, and performing at top efficiency. Then take a deep breath. What does your experience *smell* like? Does it recall a place? A mood? A particular person? If you experience this smell any time you want to, would it help you to reinforce your concentration and focus your energy? Or would it distract you? Either way, you are using this smell as a *cue*.

CUE REVIEW

What are some specific cues that you commonly respond to and which element of the mind do they trigger? Think about things that make you feel really great, that make you mad, that bring tears to your eyes, that frighten you. Use extra sheets of paper if you need to.

Cue   Mind-Part That Responds

_____   _____

_____   _____

_____   _____

_____   _____

Is there anything on this list that you would like to change? Underline it. Could the responding mind change its response? How? Is there another mind that could respond more appropriately?

In order to "change your mind"—to respond in another way—you need to know how to get in touch with each part of your mind. You can do this when you have a repertoire of cues that trigger responses from the separate parts. It's a little like having the unlisted phone numbers of several celebrities, but *you* get to make up the numbers!

What easily supplied cues are appealing to each of your minds? Here are some examples:

meeting of the minds

Executive Part: Symbols of its own ability, power and control, approval of others, achievements, skill. Will respond warmly to memories of praise and rewards for your accomplishments, to the sight of something you have created.

Wondering Part: Anything that has excited you in the past and stimulated you to explore, solve, research, thrill, dream.

Organizing Part: Symbols of order—neatly organized files, drawers, finances, possessions, ideas. Can get as excited about successful resolution (like a balanced checkbook) as the wondering part of the mind can get about a mystery.

Reacting Part: Any object or situation that is emotional, that stimulates delight, romance, contentment, joy, pleasure.

Knowing Part: Facts, physical sensations, ideas, visual images, verbal sequences (sayings, mottos, poems, etc.), sounds, music, odors, colors, tastes.

Your Personal Cues

Make a list of useful cues that appeal to your different minds.

Executive Part: _____

Wondering Part: _____

Organizing Part: _____

Reacting Part: _____

Knowing Part: _____

CHANGING YOUR MIND

The most common reason people want to switch from one part of the mind to another is when they want to be less emotional and more objective. Look especially at the cues under the reacting and organizing parts of the mind above and see if you can see a sequence.

For example, one woman was constantly tearful about her husband's painful, terminal illness. She knew this did neither of them much good, but she didn't know how to switch off the tears so she could focus on important issues. We worked out a strategy where she moved within the reacting part of her mind from her sad image, her husband lying in bed, to a happier image, her husband on their wedding day. Then she recalled how she had meticulously planned the wedding, their first home together when times were hard. A flower became her symbol of moving from one mind to another. There were the flowers of the sickroom, then the flowers of her bridal bouquet. The bridal bouquet was a double symbol of their happiness and her ability to organize and survive hard times with someone she loved. She was now operating out of the more controlled, organizing part of her mind.

What transition would you like to make? Can you design cues that will help you accomplish this?

CUE CONTRACT

Here's a mini-contract for you to consider:

The next time I encounter _____

and I start to feel _____

I will give myself this cue: _____

and I will feel _____ instead.

ARE WE
OF A MIND?

The five parts of your mind have gotten together and agreed on a course of action. Now you are trying to convince someone else. The best way is to recognize which part of his mind he is operating from. Then you can either talk directly to that part or you can try to switch him to a more accessible part.

In the *Harvard Business Review* noted clinical psychologist Dr. Carl Rogers reported that 80 percent of all verbal communication involved five types of responses. (The other 20 percent was incidental and insignificant to communication.) Intriguingly, each of Rogers's categories for verbal communication matches one of the parts of the mind:

> **Judgmental:** That's good; that's wrong. (Executive)
> **Interpretive:** You're saying that because . . . (Organizing)
> **Supportive:** I feel the same way . . . (Reacting)
> **Probing:** Where? When? (Wondering)
> **Understanding:** I understand. (Knowing)

This chapter describes clues that will help you recognize which part of the mind a person is operating from. Once you sense this, you have several options for communicating:

- Modeling—taking the position you would like her to match, speaking to her the way that you hope she will respond.

- Mirroring—matching his current position and speaking directly to that part of his mind.

- Pacing—first mirroring their current position, and then leading them to respond from a different, more appropriate position.

MODELING

Probably the most popular and traditional method of working with others is to demonstrate the behavior we would like them to have. We use "role models" for many of the facets of our lives. When you "model" while you talk to someone, you speak from the same part of the mind that you hope the other person will reply from. For instance, the modeler may be enthusiastic while the other person is depressed, calm while others lose their cool, strong when others falter. Kipling wrote a poem of tribute to modelers—"If you can keep your head when all about you are losing theirs . . ." Many self-improvement systems are based on using role models.

MIRRORING

When you want people to listen to you, you sometimes need to do more than get their attention. You need to show them that you are not threatening, that you are on their side, that you are of the same mind.

Mirroring someone's body movements, consciously or unconsciously, implies sympathy. Sit in public sometime and watch groups of people interacting. Can you tell by their body positions who agrees with whom, who disagrees? Usually those in agreement unconsciously assume the same stance, use the same gestures, move at the same tempo. Good salespeople use physical mirroring all the time, matching the energy level and body language of the potential customer to establish empathy.

If someone is agitated, depressed, defensive, tense, frantically energetic, you ally yourself with him by assuming the same position and mannerisms. When mirroring is used as part of pacing, you begin by matching someone's position, manner, actions, and then very slowly you change your pace until he follows you to new actions.

Verbal mirroring is more complex. Sensing and understanding the mood of others means moving from the part of the mind that is paying attention to you to the part that notices other people. It isn't enough to speak at the same speed or with the same expressions as the other guys. You need to identify which part of the mind they are operating out of and speak to that part. If you decide you need to talk to a different part, then you go on to "pacing," gently moving them to another operational system. Shakespeare demonstrated this brilliantly in the "Friends, Romans, countrymen . . ." speech in *Julius Caesar*. Mark Anthony stands before a crowd convinced of the justice of Julius Caesar's assassination. He agrees with them, he says. Then slowly, by citing Caesar's virtues, he turns the mob against Caesar's murderers.

PACING

There is a popular school of therapy, developed by psychologist Milton Ericson, M.D., that says "Go to where they are now and then lead them to where you want them to be." Pacing means ". . . meeting people where they are by reflecting what they know or assume to be true or by matching some part of their ongoing experience."

The pacing technique of mirroring-then-leading can be very effective in both therapeutic and everyday social and business situations. When you pace someone, you first agree that something that person already knows or does is worthwhile. Then you try to lead them to consider other possibilities. People almost always resist messages that don't match their image of the world. By establishing that you are in their corner, you increase your chances of getting them to look around at the other corners.

Pacing can take a variety of forms—physical, verbal, emotional. Experts disagree on whether or not to "pace" or mimic undesirable behavior (destructive tantrums, suicidal tendencies, violent or dishonest acts), but your good judgment should keep you from embezzlement or murder in your pursuit of your audience's attention.

To communicate, you need to offer information in a form that is acceptable to the receiver. According to Roger Peters, several studies reported in *Management Science* show that people tend to discard information when the supporting evidence isn't presented in their cognitive style. That means that if someone is working strongly from one part of the mind, an appeal to another part will probably fail. The emotional part rejects logic. The playful part rebels against executive directives. The organizer resents disruptive emotions, excessive sensory input, distraction by the imagination, and a wishy-washy or authoritarian mental executive. To communicate, imitate. If a specific communication is impossible with the viewpoint in power, try to move the person from one part of her mind to another.

First, identify where the person is. Here are some verbal clues:

"I FEEL . . ."

Because of the semantic intricacies of English, this may have three different meanings. (1) He is feeling an emotion; (2) He is experiencing a tactile (textural) or kinesthetic (space and body movement) sensation; (3) He is qualifying his statement as opinion to invite you to offer an alternative.

Response: Listen to the rest of the statement before deciding which part of the mind is at work. "I feel you're not listening to me" is probably emotional. "I feel that leaving at 7:15 will give us plenty of time to get there" is probably analytical. "I feel the painting should hang over there" is the kinesthetic division of sensory perception. "I feel this cloth is too scratchy" is an analysis of the tactile sense.

If it's a reaction from the emotions—"I feel you're not listening to me"—try responding to the emotion: "You're right. I've been too involved in this project to really hear what you are saying. Let's sit down right now [or at such-and-such a time] and we can really talk without being interrupted." Or, "You feel I'm not listening to you because I don't seem to be doing exactly what you suggest. You have some very valid points *and* I have strong feelings about the situation, too. There are some details you may not have considered. Would you like to go over them together?" ("And" is important in emotional discussions. Avoid "but.")

If the statement is analytical, respond from the organizing or knowing parts of the mind. Use cues to get you there if necessary. If the statement is from the knowing part alone, that's easy. The knowing part communicates well with all other parts of the mind.

"THIS IS AWFUL . . ."

This remark is a judgment, combined with emotions which supply blanket epithet instead of more accurate analysis.

Response: Deal with both the judgment and the emotions. Deal with the anger by offering appropriate emotional supports. Anger is often an outlet for fear of loss: loss of self-esteem ("They'll blame me"); loss of a loved one (a good example is the tearful mother of a lost child who spanks him as soon as he is found); loss of time and energy (perceived inefficiency or stupidity); loss of effort (destroying someone's work); loss of property (breaking something).

Respond to the emotional issue as you interpret it: "This is certainly not easy for you." "Don't worry, no one will blame you." "You'll get your money back." "Do you need help to fix it?" Deal with the judgmental evaluation by asking for specific details of problems and suggestions for corrections. Avoid *absolutely* a cheery, "I don't think it's so awful." This rarely works until the needs of both these parts of the mind have been met.

When someone attacks you, ask for more information. Resist the impulse to retaliate or escalate the encounter by name-calling or worse. When someone complains, don't ask what's wrong. Ask what or how it should be. In each case you are moving your opponents to the neutral ground of their Knowing Minds.

"THAT LOOKS LIKE..." "THIS SOUNDS LIKE..." "THAT FEELS LIKE..."

This by now classic trio of statements indicate that the visual, aural, and kinesthetic/tactile sensitivities are operating. (For exceptions to "feel," see page 221.)

Response: Reply to someone in the visual "mode" with visual images. Respond to verbal or aural or spatial or tactile images with the same images. Match their perceptions. (Although people sometimes say, "That smells like trouble," or "He tasted defeat," you will rarely need to deal with those senses. If you do, respond accordingly.)

"I HATE THAT"

This statement comes from the emotional reacting part, which usually fears rather than hates. "I hate arithmetic" and "I hate drunks" describe anxiety in the presence of the feared object.

Response: Deal with the "hate" (fear) as an emotion. Logic is useless until the fear has been acknowledged: "Numbers are so confusing, almost as difficult as those jigsaw puzzles [or road maps or recipes or conference schedules] you do so well. How do you know what to do with all those symbols?" Or, "Yes, you never know what a drunk is going to do. They're really scary. I knew someone . . ." and a sympathetic anecdote turns the abstract "drunk" back into a real person who is inebriated.

CHANGING SOMEONE'S MIND

If someone is being highly judgmental, stuck in the mental executive mode with a *Manual of Procedures* that needs to be updated, you may want to lead her to the emotional reacting part of her mind so she can empathize with you or others. You could try impassioned appeals to her emotions, but you know how far that got the charity solicitors with Ebenezer Scrooge. Lacking Dickens's three Christmas ghosts, you'll do better with a three-step maneuver: (1) Engage the organizing part of her mind with analytic data; (2) Work your quarry over to the neutral knowing part of her mind by concentrating on background information and shared experiences; (3) When she has stopped being critical and is no longer operating from the critical executive part of her mind, progress to the reacting part of her mind.

If someone is highly emotional, you can join him and then gently lead him to a more neutral ground. Suppose someone is really upset, at you or something else. He's shouting, waving his arms around, red in the face. You can try remaining placid and unmoved until he calms down. Or you can join him in denouncing the *situation*, not the people involved: "Oh, God! That's horrible! How could that have happened! I'll never get over this! This is so stupid!" By matching his energy, you acknowledge that this is indeed an emotional issue. Then you slowly calm down, leading him to where you both can assess the situation more realistically.

BODY LANGUAGE

"Reading" body language is a popular pastime, but the meaning of body language and eye contact are not the same everywhere or to everyone. The American ideal of looking your listener straight in the eye can get you in a lot of trouble with people of different cultural backgrounds. Certain gestures also have vastly different meanings to different age groups and nationalities. If a northern Italian is shaking his head slowly as you speak, he disagrees with you. If a southern Italian nods his head, he also disagrees. A Portuguese who tugs his ear is saying, "You're right," but an Italian using the same gesture would be questioning your sexual orientation. Displaying the palms of your hands to your listener is the ultimate insult in Greece, but American women unconsciously thrust their open palms toward people with whom they feel complete agreement. Arms crossed on the chest may mean disagreement or defensiveness when done by a young man, excitement and agreement when done by an older woman. Whatever the "message" of body position, if you begin by mirroring it you are putting yourself in the same kinesthetic space as your listener.

WORKING AS PART OF A TEAM

You *can* work effectively, even joyously with people who are operating from other parts of their minds than you are. Collaboration can be a team effort in which each person offers different perspectives. Effective business teams often consist of an innovator/artist/inventor (wondering part) and an organizer/manager (organizing part). Marriage partnerships usually involve two people with different skills who mesh their strengths and weaknesses in powerful symbiosis.

When partners have very different ways of operating, they run two risks:

1. One may decide he can no longer function alone. Any threat to the partnership will seem catastrophic.

2. In times of stress, either partner may denigrate the other for working differently or lacking the same perceptions.

But advantages are many, and so partnership is a joyous and fulfilling way of working for most of us. It multiplies energy, perspectives, possibilities. Some noted collaborations include Rodgers and Hammerstein, Masters and Johnson, Lily Tomlin and Jane Wagner, the Kennedy family, John and Abigail Adams, and the Ewings of TV's *Dallas*.

In any group, family, or business, tasks are divided. Sometimes the structure dictates that certain group members can operate from only a few of their minds. This works nicely until someone objects. A few folks can go through life never making a decision or responding emotionally or learning something new. But most of us want a full repertoire of mind activity. The assembly line worker who never gets to choose or plan quickly burns out. The wife who is afraid to reveal her managerial talents, the husband who is afraid to reveal his feelings are both likely to sour on their restricted roles. Anyone who either turns off one of his minds or hides its activity is trying to fly a jet on low octane.

Unfortunately, limiting which minds we use is not uncommon. It happens not only in communication between the sexes, generations, employer and employee, but even between political, religious, and social factions.

MEETING OF THE MINDS

Sara and Jack seemed an ideal couple, but there were unseen tensions below the surface. Whenever Sara would "unload" on Jack at the end of a hard day, he would jump in with vigorous solutions to all the "problems" she presented. Sara didn't actually want resolutions for most of her complaints, only sympathy, someone to share the events of the day and validate her responses to them. Jack was equally frustrated. Sara didn't "listen" to him—or at least didn't rush to carry out his wise solutions to her dilemmas. And when he described problems at work, she didn't make suggestions. Instead she offered soothing support for his ego—"You're a great person to put up with all that." At home Sara would politely drop circuitous hints about what she needed from Jack, but sometimes he failed to respond. Jack in turn would give clear orders, and Sara would carry them out, occasionally with a sullen, harassed expression.

Each of them was acting and reacting in ways that their *Manual of Procedures* said were correct. Jack "knew" he should ignore any messages that conflicted with those from the logical, judgmental part of his mind. Sara "knew" she should ignore messages from the analytic part of her mind in favor of emotional information.

Neither Jack nor Sara realized that they were trying to communicate from different minds. Both were shortchanging themselves by limiting their repertoire of responses. Despite decades of new awareness of sex roles, men and women who step outside this old, society-imposed stereotype can still encounter vigorous hostility—"She's too masculine/pushy/cold/hard." "He's too soft/weak/effeminate/wimpy."

So Jack and Sara simply plugged along. His image of her as inept and ineffectual was constantly reinforced, while in Sara's eyes, Jack grew more and more unfeeling and dictatorial. Here was a classic case of the analytic organizing part of the mind in collision with the emotional reacting part.

Sara understood the dilemma more quickly than Jack. She discovered the consciousness-raising ideology of the 1960s just 20 years late and began to change her perspective. Jack reacted as anyone does in the midst of major change. He was alarmed, confused, angry. Sara could have regarded Jack as the enemy and lashed out at him, but she realized that he had been victimized just as much as she had.

Her first step was to interact with Jack as a partner when he was operating from the organizing or executive parts of his mind. This meant changing her response to his instructions from sullen compliance to active and cheerful discussion of options and alternate methods. Since this change could be quite threatening, she also decided not to "dump" her problems on Jack unless she wanted to discuss solutions. She had now moved over to operating from the organizing and executive parts of her mind, while still trying to provide Jack with the emotional support he needed to get through this big change.

Having "gone to where he was," she began trying to move him to where she wanted him to be—that is, to get Jack to acknowledge messages from his sensory system and his emotions. Their discussions moved to areas that had always been considered her private territory—decorating their home, managing social engagements, communicating with relatives. He had felt that time spent on these activities was wasted. She tried to demonstrate how concerning himself with his support structure could be pleasurable and actually save him time and inconvenience. She sought his assistance in handling sensitive personal interactions, in deciding which friends to ask to a party, in arranging the furniture, in planning the events that made up their life together. Jack proved to have an extremely fine eye for color and found he remembered a color exactly when matching paint chips and carpeting.

Jack and Sara could have gone on forever as partners, happily filling the gaps in each other's repertoires. However, Sara decided that she wanted to expand her mind power. Instead of breaking up the partnership so she would be free to use all parts of her mind, she looked for ways to change the task assignments within the partnership. She chose a difficult middle path, but it let her enjoy the benefits of using all parts of her mind and of being part of a team.

Identify the technique or techniques that you are using to communicate:

_____   1. He crosses his arms. You cross your arms. He strokes his ear. You stroke your ear.

_____   2. She is heartbroken, sobbing. You cry with her, tell her the same thing has happened to you. Then you begin asking questions about the situation. Finally you ask her what her next step will be.

_____   3. She is heartbroken, sobbing. You sit quietly until she is calmer, then ask her what her next step will be.

_____   4. He is furious with you, swinging fists and chairs as he approaches. You say, "Boy, are you upset! This is awful! The most terrible thing I've ever seen! How could something like that happen! You look mad as hell!"

_____   5. He is furious with you. You say, "This is terrible! It's all ruined! It shouldn't look like that at all. How should it look? What can I do to fix it? I'll start immediately."

_____   6. She is nervous, twitching, unable
                      to sit still, talking so fast that she
                      barely finishes one sentence before
                      starting another. You sit quietly
                      until she calms down.

_____   7. He is nervous, twitching, unable to
                      sit still. You tell him how nervous
                      you are, that this kind of thing
                      makes you practically faint. He's
                      holding up very well, you think.
                      You're starting to calm down
                      already, talking to him like this.

Answers

　1. Mirroring

　2. Pacing

　3. Modeling

　4. Mirroring

　5. Pacing

　6. Modeling

　7. Pacing

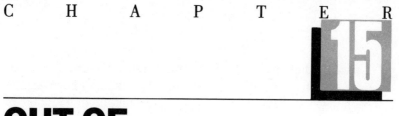

C H A P T E R

15

OUT OF
YOUR MIND

Do I contradict myself? Very well then I contradict myself. (I am large, I contain multitudes.)

—Walt Whitman, *Leaves of Grass*

Your mind is working all the time. Why not help it to work *for* you? Your multiple-part mind—for all its faults—is capable of providing everything you need when you need it, out of its own infinitely rich resources. Its complexity, contrariness, and contradictions are what separate you from and *elevate you above* computers.

Computers don't think. They are morons, able to choose between on/off or yes/no in complex patterns and at lightning fast speed. In some cases, their process resembles the human thought process. But computers are simply high tech slaves. They have many of the same advantages and disadvantages as human slaves would—they do things we don't care to bother with, quickly and efficiently, but they can also be temperamental and costly, they sometimes break down, and maddeningly they insist on giving us what we ask for rather than what we sometimes really want. For all their aura of omniscience, they are still slaves. Kurt Vonnegut, Jr., warned us in his novel *Player Piano* that "anybody that competes with slaves becomes a slave."

Despite their occasional goofs, computers lack one tremendous advantage that we humans possess: We can make brilliant mistakes. In his book *The Cult of Information*, Theodore Roszak quotes astronomer Sir Bernard Lovell: "I fear that literal-minded, narrowly focused computerized research is proving antithetical to the free exercise of that happy faculty known as serendipity." A prime example of mental serendipity is what cultural historian Roszak calls the *master idea*.

MASTER IDEAS

Roszak says, "Master ideas are based on no information whatever." He cites examples: "All men are created equal." "God is love." " Life is a meaningless absurdity." None of these ideas can be proven or disproven. They are simply accepted or rejected. Accepted, they have the power to shape history and form our concept of self. Rejected, they pass quickly into oblivion. People are frequently willing to kill (or be killed) to support (or reject) Master Ideas. Master Ideas affect the philosophy, religious belief, literature, arts, and laws of a society. No computer ever had a Master Idea. These ideas are what the human minds are about.

Where do Master Ideas come from? Probably no individual or committee could sit down and come up with one to order. They arise by spontaneous generation out of the immensely complex, protean brain debris that we refer to as "knowledge." No knowledge, no idea. "Perhaps this volatility of mind," says Roszak, "is what saves human society from the changeless rigidity of the other social animals, the ants, the bees, the beasts of the pack and herd. We are gifted as a species with a crowning tangle of electrochemical cells which has become an idea-maker."

DESCARTES AND THE ANGEL OF TRUTH

When 23-year-old Frenchman Rene Descartes lay down to sleep on the night of November 10, 1619, he had already absorbed a lot of knowledge about the world as the seventeenth century knew it. That night the "Angel of Truth" appeared to him in three dazzling dreams. This insight set him to writing "Rules for the Direction of the Mind."

Read casually today, Descartes' "rules" seem somewhat clichéd, more like commonsense statements that almost anyone could have come up with. But in the seventeenth century, common sense viewed the world and our place in it quite differently.

Descartes' idea was to find axioms, clear statements that no one could doubt, and then link them together to form simple, sensible, self-evident rules. Using this systematic method, he reasoned, would expand our body of knowledge. (This was pretty daring stuff in an era when discussing ideas could mean burning at the stake or worse. Descartes himself went into exile and didn't publish any of his work until late in his life.)

Descartes' work led to modern philosophy and to analytic geometry which is the basis of modern mathematics. Curiously, the one element that he left out of his careful sequences was his own "angel," the flash of inspiration, the light bulb that goes on and lets us suddenly see familiar things in a new light.

TYRANNY OR RICHES?

Each of our multiple selves is a petty tyrant. . . . We are not totalitarian states but banana republics, with juntas ruling more or less effectively, constantly threatened with revolution by strong opposing factions. . . .

—Roger Peters, *Practical Intelligence*

You can view the conflicting needs of your mind as painfully insoluble, constant sources of friction, disruption, and even anarchy. Or you can "reframe" your view of your mental diversity, choosing to see the parts of your mind as a broadly talented support group providing almost infinite resources for enriching your life.

"It has begun to be recognized," say Ornstein and Sobel, "that a person in the face of all this instability, wild change, and tumult is not powerless: He or she already *has a brain* that possesses the evolved network of 500 million years of nerve circuits that can deal with the continual changes." What other device can claim 500 million years of constant improvements? The brain and its associated mind may not be perfect, but it is darn close!

Balzac said proudly, "In my five feet three inches I contain every possible inconsistency and contrast." Learn to glory in your contrasts. Cherish your inconsistency. Like a Stradivarius violin, your mind may never reveal exactly how it does what it does, but the music is just as magnificent. Theodore Roszak says, "The art of thinking is grounded in the mind's astonishing capacity to create beyond what it intends, beyond what it can foresee." Be alive to that dimension beyond the foreseen.

BOOKS AND MINDS

Can reading this book or any book suddenly unlock all your potential? The printed word is powerful, but perhaps not that powerful. Self-help books are just that—guidelines for helping yourself. "Do not expect to pick up a paperback at the airport, read it, and thereby shed your neuroses," says Stanford engineer James L. Adams in his book *Conceptual Blockbusting*. "However," he adds, "many of these books will at least cause you to think."

In this book you have explored some ways to think, some ways to make your multifaceted mind "mind." You've viewed your mind as simultaneously potent, whimsical, and vulnerable. Together, the diverse and sometimes contradictory parts of your mind have the power to learn and create, to heal and imagine, to sustain life and sanity and purpose in the face of terrific odds. With your permission, they can also serve as a tool to glimpse the infinite.

INDEX

Rodale Press, Inc., publishes PREVENTION®, the better health magazine.
For information on how to order your subscription,
write to PREVENTION®, Emmaus, PA 18098.